A Most Unlikely Servant

Elizabeth Lane

A Most Unlikely Servant
by Elizabeth Lane

Printed in the United States of America

ISBN 1-60034-521-2

www.xulonpress.com

Bible Reference Page

New American Standard Bible
Red Letter Edition
Concordance
Copyright © 1960, 1962, 1963, 1968, 1971, 1972, 1973,
1975, 1977
Publisher: Holman

The Quest Study Bible
New International Version
Copyright © 1999
Publisher: Zondervan

Life Application Study Bible
New Living Translation
Copyright © 1988, 1989, 1990, 1991, 1993, 1996
Publisher: Tyndale

Crossings Devotional Bible
King James Version
Copyright © 2001
Publisher: Crossings Book Club
Garden City, New York

Positive Thinking Bible
Contemporary English Version
Copyright © 1998
Publisher: Nelson

This book is dedicated to my Savior the Lord Jesus Christ
for without Him my life would not be possible.

I would like to thank my family, church family,
and friends for all the support and encouragement they
provided me over the years. A special thanks to the lady
who took her time to read my manuscript and for her
encouragement and support.

Note: Some of the names of the characters and locations
have been changed to protect their identity and privacy.

Introduction

Do you feel like your life is going nowhere? Are you stuck in a rut? Or are you just existing? Come with me and take a journey through my life in search of a better life. Walk with me through the trials and tribulations of growing up in a large family. Come see the world through the eyes of a child and learn the deep dark secret that one day awakened my heart. Journey with me through the struggles I faced as a victim of abuse. See how my heart so longed for a relationship with my mother and what I found in search of a mother.

My prayer for you is that when you take this journey through my life you will see the need for the better life. I have traveled on both sides of the road—in both darkness and light. I have run into many detours along the way. But, one thing I know for sure is that the road I traveled in the light is the better life - the light that lead to a personal relationship with the Lord Jesus Christ. I would like to invite you now to see what a difference my personal relationship with Jesus Christ made in my life.

In the hollow of His hand
He will hide me
When the storms of life sweep by.

Florence Jones Hadley

Chapter 1

In the beginning…

"Before I formed you in the womb, I knew you, before you were born I set you apart…" Jeremiah 1:5

EXTRA! EXTRA! READ ALL ABOUT IT…
CLOUDY & COOLER, POSSIBLE AFTERNOON
SHOWERS, LOW 45, HIGH 53.
WEATHER DETAILS ON P. 26.
HOPES FOR BERLIN SETTLEMENT RISE
MARIS BAGS 61ST HR FOR NEW SEASON RECORD
DOWNIE QUITS PORT POSITION FOR BUSINESS
EGYPT CUTS JORDAN, TURK TIES
BUCS WIN, 3-1
STEELERS LOSE TO LA RAMS 24-14
TROPICAL STORM FRANCES MAKES HER WAY
ACROSS THE CARIBBEAN

These headlines made front page news for Monday, October 2, 1961, as reported in the *Pittsburgh Post-Gazette*. There was not much happening in the news, just what seemed like an ordinary day. But on this day in a small town just outside of Pittsburgh, my parents were awaiting my arrival. According to my mother, there were some complications surrounding my birth, but I do not know exactly what they were. My mother told me that my father was going to have to choose between me and her, but then I was born. Weighing in at a healthy 8 pounds, 3 ounces, I made my way into the world. Of course, I was an adorable, cuddly, and pleasant baby. I had beautiful blue eyes, a bald head, and I was a little on the chubby side. I think I was probably my mother's biggest baby. Mom said that some of the people on staff at the hospital wanted to keep me; however, a big welcoming committee was waiting for me at home. At birth, my mother named me Betty Ann, and I became the tenth child of what would soon be twelve children.

All my life our family lived in a small town outside of Pittsburgh. We lived in a three-story home with a cellar. My parents were of Slovak and Hungarian descent. Their religion was Greek Catholic. So, naturally, I would be raised Greek Catholic. Both of my parents came from large families. Dad was one of fourteen children, and Mom was the oldest of eight children. Dad and Mom were middle-class, blue-collar workers. I considered our family to be an average, normal family. Growing up, my parents did not talk much about their parents. Mom used to tell us about my dad's mother and say how wonderful she was, but she never talked about her parents. As a matter of fact, I never saw a picture of my mom's mother and father until I was in my late twenties. My paternal grandfather came to America from Russia when he was about fifteen years old. He would be the only grandparent I knew, but I did not know him very well. My other grandparents died before I was born.

Dad was a quiet, simple man, and a passive alcoholic. He was a postal worker. Some of my brothers and sisters might say that my father didn't talk too much to us. But my perception of my dad was different than that of my brothers and sisters. Dad did talk to me, but sometimes I had to initiate the conversation. He loved to talk about history and I loved to hear his stories. So, history was usually our topic of choice. Dad also did daily meal preparation for our family before he went to work, because he worked the second shift. My father didn't like chaos. My perception of his philosophy as he would say was, "Let sleeping dogs lie," because he wanted to keep peace in the house. Although my father was a quiet man and didn't say too much about anything, he knew everything you did. For instance, one of my older sisters, Gracie, went to a club one night. I would guess she didn't tell my parents where she was going. The next morning, my father handed her the morning paper. In a front page article, it was reported that a young man was shot in front of the club Gracie was at the night before. Needless to say, my dad didn't have to say a word to her. Later, Gracie told me that she had left the club a short time before the shooting occurred. I'm sure she was shocked that my father knew where she was. If dad had to reprimand you for something, which was something he didn't do often, then you knew you were in serious trouble. When I was young, my little brother, his friend, and I used to go fishing, and play on the barges down on the river. I didn't know that my dad knew that we played on the barges at the river. One day, my father told me that we shouldn't be playing down there, because it wasn't safe. As I think back, I guess I didn't think I could get hurt. Now, I remember that my dad lost his oldest brother, who was about twelve, to that river. His brother fell off the bridge and drowned.

Dad graduated salutatorian of his high school class. He was a World War II veteran. He did not share much about serving in the war with us, but he enjoyed getting together with his old Army buddies at the annual reunion for war veterans. In his later years, Dad liked going to wrestling matches with his uncle. Dad didn't like to go far away from home or travel, but did on rare occasions. He didn't have hobbies or collections. He was just a plain, simple man.

Mom, I believe, was the only one in her family first to complete school, and then go on for higher education. She was the boss – a perfectionist, controlling, artistic, and creative. She liked to bake pastries, help other people, travel, and go to flea markets. My mother didn't have any collections that I know of, but I think remodeling our house was her hobby. Growing up, we could have had our own remodeling business, because my mother usually had us remodeling something in our house. Our house was about seventy-five years old when our family moved into it. It still had a coal furnace. So, I'm sure our house was in need of some basic repairs. My two oldest brothers had a race car. They painted the logo "Mom's Home Remodeling" on the side of it. They also gave her a plaque with the same logo on it. That's how much she liked to remodel.

Mom's perfectionistic ways could be seen in the house-keeping. Every Saturday was cleaning day. We (the children) had to be up at approximately 6:00 a.m. to begin cleaning. If we weren't up by 6:00 a.m., my mother would holler up the steps to make sure we were getting up. At times, I am sure that the whole neighborhood would be awakened by my mother's holler. My sister Charity would say that my mom called only her name to get out of bed, but we were right behind her. Charity was in charge of Saturday cleaning. And we didn't just do surface cleaning. The cleaning had to be thorough. You cleaned, scrubbed, and moved everything. Sometimes you would have to use a toothbrush to clean things between the cracks or whatever it took to get the job done. I would consider Saturday cleaning more like spring cleaning. If the cleaning wasn't done to meet my mother's expectations, then you were surely going to hear about it. One day, when we were still teenagers, my mother must have been complaining that the house was not clean enough. I remember my brother Tim was upset that my mother was not happy with our cleaning and commented that even his friends thought we had the cleanest house around. Considering all the traffic we had coming in and out of the house, I think we kept a pretty clean house.

My mother was a Licensed Professional Nurse, and she was very particular and perfectionistic about the way her work clothes were washed. As tradition held, each daughter would get her turn in being responsible for washing and ironing my mother's uniform and polishing her shoes for work. At that time, my mom wore the traditional white nursing uniform, white nursing hat, and white nursing shoes. One day, when I was in charge of getting her work clothes ready for work, I did not polish her shoes white enough, and the shoe strings were not white enough. I know there were quite a few times I did not do her clothes and shoes to perfection. I remember my mother got very angry with me and started screaming at me saying she was going to be late for work, because I did not polish her shoes well enough. She took the shoes over to the kitchen sink and ripped the shoe strings out of the shoes. My mother repolished the shoes and shoe laces to make them perfectly white. Eventually, my uniform washing days came to an end.

For my parents, raising a large family brought about many challenges, especially financial. Mom was head of the household and in charge of the finances. I believe my parents had a retirement plan through my dad's work, but I don't think they had a savings account. Needless to say, they lived paycheck to paycheck and struggled financially all their life. When it came time to pay the bills, I remember Mom always saying she had to "rob Peter to pay Paul," but somehow she managed. Our family had the basic needs met (i.e. food, water, and a roof over our head etc.), but I would consider us poor. My parents weren't always able to buy us new things (i.e. shoes, pants etc.). I remember my mother bought me a training bra, a bra you usually got before you got the real bra, when I was about ten years old. I didn't get a real bra until I was in ninth grade. I bought it myself and I only had one. If you got a new pair of two dollar shoes from the D & K Store, an equivalent to that of the Dollar Store today, then you were really in style. I loved wearing my new D & K white tennis shoes. To me, I would consider D & K tennis shoes to be comparable to Nikes or Addidas today. We got hand-me-downs from older brothers and sisters. Sometimes, people our family or relatives knew would provide us with clothing, toys, and things they didn't need or want anymore. I liked getting hand-me-downs and I still do today.

From my perspective, there were assigned daily job positions in our home when I was young. This is my perception of job distributions; Charity was the acting "mom" in charge; Faith was the cook; Gracie was the dish washer, and Susan, Hope, and I were the dish dryers. My oldest sister Jean only lived with us at times, so she probably assumed the "in charge" position. Now, the boys played the traditional role of males at that time, doing yard work, taking out garbage, etc. Also, some of my older brothers did the cooking at some point in their growing up.

One night, when I was older I had just come from an evening out with friends and was quite intoxicated: I told my parents they reminded me of "Ma and Pa Kettle." Let me explain who Ma and Pa were for those of you who don't know. "Ma and Pa Kettle" was a series of movies that was on television back in the early days of my life. They lived on a run-down, old farm with lots of children (maybe even more than we had) and animals. Ma, Pa, and family were a pitiful sight, but they were funny. Ma's hair and clothing were always in disarray. As for Pa, he just did what Ma said to do. The only difference between our family and Ma and Pa Kettle's was that they lived on a farm and we lived in the city; we probably could have used a farm.

I was born and raised to the sounds of Motown. My sisters, some brothers, and I loved to sing and dance to the sounds of Motown. My sister Susan, Hope, and I were able to take some Jazz and Tap lessons when I young. I loved to dance. Singing and dancing were soothing and comforting to my soul. Singing and dancing allowed me to escape from the everyday challenges.

In the fall, it was back to school, going to bed early, and doing homework. Our bedtime was usually between 7:30 p.m. and 8:00 p.m. My favorite uncle would visit us on Thursday, which was one of my dad's days off at that time. My uncle used to bring quite a few loaves of bread and big giant chocolate chip cookies (and I tell you the truth they were big) from Vienna Bakery. Thursday was a day we looked forward to. We enjoyed seeing my uncle come to our house and so did some of the neighborhood kids. We couldn't wait to eat the chocolate chip cookies, which were such a treat. Desserts were a rare occasion in our house. When I moved to Georgia, I had to get use to eating desserts, because people here eat them with at least a couple of meals on an everyday basis. I can still smell the sweet aroma of my dad's homemade pumpkin and/or cherry pies, and tootsie rolls that usually marked the beginning of fall for me. I looked forward to coming home from school, seeing my dad on his days off, and eating his homemade pies. The tootsie rolls went fast so you had to be there when they came out of the oven or you didn't get any.

Wintertime brought outdoor activities such as snowballs fights, building igloos, and sled riding. There was a big, steep, cobblestone hill across the street from our house we called "Steepy." This was the place to be in the winter for sled riding. Steepy was about a mile long or so. All the kids in the neighborhood would meet there to sled ride. We didn't have snowsuits to suit up in, and many times we were without gloves and hats. So, we used socks to warm our hands, and extra shirts and pants to keep warm. Nor did we have the neat sleds or other costly sled-riding gear that some people had, so we used plastic bags or a piece of tin to sled ride. Then, we would walk to the top of Steepy and slide down. At times, we would pile as many as three people high lying on one piece of plastic to make the ride to the bottom. Sometimes, we would build a slope of snow toward the bottom of the hill. As you traveled down the hill you picked up speed. When you hit the slope, you would go sailing in the air across the road and down the next hill. It was so much fun. Indoor activities would include playing board games and pretend church, school or store.

Holidays in our house were usually busy, fun, and at times joyless. Christmastime was the busiest. 'Tis the season to decorate the house, eat lots of desserts, and listen to holiday music. My mom would spend many weeks making an assorted array of pastries and preparing for Christmas. Having such a large family, I don't know how my parents managed to make sure they didn't forget to get someone a gift or how they were able to afford all the gifts. As our family grew, so did the celebration. We had enough family members to make every holiday seem like one big party. Food was plentiful and there were usually foods that we didn't get to have all the time. One of my nieces thought that every time she came to grandma and grandpa's house we were celebrating a birthday. So, at Christmas my mom decided to get a birthday cake to celebrate Jesus' birthday. Personally, my favorite holiday was Thanksgiving, because it was not so materialistic. You could just enjoy dinner and each other's company without all the commercialism. Holidays sometimes were also a sad time at our house. My mom would spend a lot of time preparing for the holidays, but when the day came she appeared to not want to be part of the family get-together and to not want to spend time with us. On the day of the holiday, my mom would usually pretend to be sick, spend the day in bed or do a disappearing act (She would sneak out of the house and go visit other people.), or sometimes she would even go into one of her rages, which usually made the holiday very sad and gloomy. Even today, my mom still wants to be pretty much on her own, usually spending time with other people, instead of our family.

Springtime brought about the heavenly scent of blooming flowers, fresh cut grass, eating home-grown corn on the cob, watermelon, and playing jump rope. Penny candy was a sign of the times and eating sunflower seeds was a tradition. For the most part, if you ate sunflower seeds (and that would be pretty much all the kids on the street who did it), then you knew how to eat them like the pros. You put a handful of seeds in your mouth, sucked the salt off them, cracked open the seed with your teeth, ate the seed, and spit the shell out of your mouth on the ground.

My uncle George lived in another state and would come to visit us on occasion. Uncle George's visit meant water gun fights. My uncle would bring a large supply of water guns, and the water battles would begin. I am sure my parents were not too keen on our squirting water all over the place, but we did it anyway. Springtime also marked the beginning of the end of school and the start of summer.

Summertime meant vacation and being out of school, but family vacations were not a luxury we were able to afford. However, we were able to go to amusement parks, and have cookouts and picnics. My dad's company sponsored annual picnics at an amusement park called Rainbow Gardens. When I was little, going to my dad's annual company picnic was the highlight of my summer. Also, summertime was a time of playing outdoors. Since our house was located on the corner of a four-way intersection, the neighborhood kids would meet on the corner to get together to play baseball, kickball, and handball. Our favorite game was handball. We would be up at the crack of dawn, playing ball until the sun went down. Then, we might switch to games like hide and seek or release the den. Sometimes, my favorite uncle would take some of us kids to the duck pond to feed the ducks. The duck pond was actually located in a cemetery. After we fed the ducks, everyone, including my uncle, would climb up the hill in the cemetery and just lie down and roll all the way down the hill. It didn't take much for us to have plain, simple fun. My brother Drew would sometimes borrow my uncle's pick-up truck, pile some of us and some of the neighborhood kids in the back of the pick-up and go for long rides. Being indoors was not a place we wanted to be in the summer. Our town had a curfew. At 10:00 p.m. all the children had to be off the streets. The police station whistle blew at 9:45 p.m. for a warning to let us know that it was almost time to be in the house. Then at 10:00 p.m. the whistle blew again, and the police usually made rounds to make sure that the kids were off the street and in the house, but sometimes we still tried to hang out on the corner. Sometimes, our family was able to do other miscellaneous activities, such as ice skating, roller skating, swimming, or going to drive-in movies, but funds were not always available.

In spite of being financially challenged, my parents somehow managed to provide a Catholic education for all of us, at least through elementary school. Some of my brothers and sisters attended Catholic school through middle school and a few years into high school. Growing up, my parents were very religious and strict, especially my dad. For example, during Lent our religion required that on Good Friday you keep as silent as you can between noon and 3:00 p.m. This silent time was in honor of Jesus' death. I remember one Good Friday; I guess I was not being quiet, and my dad told me to sit down and be still. He said that I was not allowed to listen to the radio, watch TV or anything; just be quiet.

When I was young, my dad did not like us to clean the house or wash clothes on Sunday. It was God's day and you were supposed to rest, according to the Bible. In the book of Exodus, Chapter 31, Verse 15 it says: "For six days, work is to be done, but the seventh day is a Sabbath of rest." I'm sure there were many times when obeying this law was not possible, but dad tried to uphold this tradition the best he could. I know as we got older and times changed there were many things that had to be done on Sundays. I miss the good old days when businesses were closed on Sundays and you had nothing else to do but spend time with your family. My parents tried to make sure you were following the rules of Catholicism. All my brothers were altar boys. We practiced all the traditions and rituals, according to the Catholic Church. Our church observed all Holy Days and holidays. That meant you were expected to be at church every time there was a Mass. Dad and Mom were also "transportation-ally" challenged. Mom never learned to drive a car. They had only one car for fourteen people. Go ahead and try to figure out that seating arrangement. Now work with me; we have one car and fourteen people. No problem, we could have gone in shifts. You know, take a load of kids to the designated destination and keep coming back until we were all accounted for. Of course, public transportation and walking were a familiar source of transportation. If we ever complained about walking, my dad would always tell us about the many miles he walked to and from school every day in all kinds of weather. Anyway, I'm not sure how my parents managed to get us all to the same place, but they did. I know they did the best they could with what they had.

Although we had what some people might consider a big house, it was small for the size of our family. We had three floors and a cellar. The first floor had a living room and dining room area, a nice sized kitchen, a hallway, and a bath on the first floor when our family first moved into the house. The second floor had four or five rooms, but they were not very big. The house had an attic that had two rooms and what I would consider a half room. Sleeping arrangements were as follows: my parents and the girls occupied the second floor and the boys occupied the attic. You usually had to share a bed (sometimes with anywhere from three to five people) and bedroom with some of the other children. Sometimes, you had to sleep on the floor or wherever you could find a space. Having only one full bath in our house was quite a challenge at times. In the cellar, we had a make-shift shower, in time a toilet, and limited hot water. And when I say make-shift shower, that is exactly what it was – a shower head for the water to come out and the cement floor. The toilet just sat over a sewer; it was not grounded. And if I remember correctly, you had to pour water into it to make it flush. I'm sure there was a lot of praying going on at bath time. Eventually, the first floor bathroom was moved to the second floor and the bathroom on the first floor was made into a laundry room and half bathroom. To this day, I still do not know how we all managed to get use of the bathroom and survive. Needless to say, bath time was always a challenge for our family.

Along with the limited supply of hot water was a limited supply of heat. We had a furnace in the cellar, but it could only heat the cellar and the first floor of our house. When I was growing up, Pittsburgh had some seriously cold winters with lots of snow and days of below zero weather. So, this made getting ready for bed in the winter a chore. Now, if you're like most people you just put a pair of pajamas on and go to bed. Right? Well, in our house it was more like Operation Bedtime. Putting on your pajamas was only the first step in getting ready for bed. Next, you would put on a second layer of clothes (i.e. preferably, sweatshirts and/or sweatpants). Caution! If you put too many clothes on, then you might risk the chance of sweating and this was not in your best interest. Third, you would put on your socks and gloves. Coats, hats, and scarves were optional, but sometimes necessary. The fourth step was to make sure you had as many blankets (from a limited supply) as you could find, even if that meant you had to take them from someone else. Now, you were ready to take the bedtime plunge. The last and final step was to jump into bed, get under the blankets, and pull the blankets over your head. Pulling the blankets over your head was to make sure you stayed as warm as possible. And you probably thought I was kidding about bedtime being a chore. My parents did not get a furnace put in our upstairs until I was in my early twenties.

Dinnertime at our house was first come, first served, meaning that if you didn't come to dinner when you were called, then the food selection was slim picking or none. If you missed dinner or just wanted a midnight snack and were outside late at night, sometimes you might see the boys reeling a large bag on a rope with pizza and food in it up the side of our house to the attic on the third floor. I think that it was a pretty good assumption that the boys did this so that they didn't have to share their food. My older brothers and sisters still talk about our sister Faith and how she would get up early in the morning before everyone else, just to get first choice of the food. One thing that I really appreciated about my parents was that even though we didn't have much food they would, without a thought, offer food to anyone who stopped by to visit us. I recall a story that our neighbor Mrs. Mills told me about my nephew Paul. My parents had custody of Paul and his sister. Mrs. Mills said she had come over to our house to visit my mother, but my mother was not at home. Mrs. Mills said that Paul told her to come into the house, and my mother would be home soon. Now, Paul was only eight or nine years old. Paul asked Mrs. Mills if she would like a Jumbo (Jumbo is another name for bologna, for those of you who are not from Pittsburgh.) sandwich or something to eat and drink. If Mrs. Mills wanted something to eat then he was going to make it for her. You learned at an early age to ask company if they wanted something to eat. Mrs. Mills thought this was the sweetest thing for Paul to offer to make her something to eat. Occasionally some of my friends would call me and ask me what we were having for dinner. Then they would come over to our house at dinner time to get something to eat, because they knew they could. My family did not have a lot of food, but what we had we shared. I often wonder how we ever had enough food to feed all of us and then some. This brings to my mind the story in the book of Matthew, Chapter 14. Jesus fed the 5,000 people with only five loaves of bread and two small fish and still had twelve baskets of food left over. Even though my family wasn't Christian, I believe that God had his hand on our family. I know for sure that God had his hand on me.

Chapter 2

A Strong-Willed Child

"No longer will you be called Abram; your name will be
Abraham." Genesis 17:5

I love the story about Abraham, particularly the faith he
had to believe that God would make him the "father of
many nations." After God called Abraham to serve Him, He
made a covenant with Abraham. As part of that covenant,
God changed his name from Abram to Abraham. It was not
uncommon for God to change the name of the people He
called to serve Him. For example, Abraham's wife Sarai's
name was changed to Sarah; Jacob's name was changed to
Israel; and Saul's name was changed to Paul.

Remember, I said earlier my mother named me Betty
Ann. Well, shortly after my birth my name was changed. I
was baptized a couple of weeks after I was born, which was
according to Catholic custom. According to Catholic ordinance, your first and middle name had to be a saint's name.
The name Betty did not meet the Catholic ordinance criteria.
So, the priest who baptized me changed my name to Elizabeth

Ann, without my parents' consent. My mother told me she didn't change my name back to Betty. Elizabeth Ann is my legal name and the name I believe God wanted me to have. I feel honored with the way my name came to be. One time, I bought a name card at a Christian book store that had the meaning of the name Elizabeth on it. The card said Elizabeth means "consecrated to God" or "set apart to do God's work." John 15:16 says, "You did not choose me, I chose you." Even as a baby, I believe God chose me to serve Him.

Growing up in a large family, you got lost in the shuffle very easily. With both of my parents working, I was often left in the care of older brothers and sisters. It was a fight for the survival of the fittest. Sometimes, the babysitter or the person watching you did not keep a close eye on you. Let me tell you about my scar. One day when I was about ten or eleven years old, my mother, for some reason out the blue, told me about the scar that is under my left breast. I knew that the scar was there. I never questioned why I had the scar, because I thought it was normal. Anyway, my mother said when I was still an infant my older sister Gracie was playing doctor and took a knife and started cutting into my chest. The cut was pretty close to my heart. I am not sure who was supposed to be watching me, but they did not do a good job. I did not suffer any permanent damage, just a scar.

As a child, I had to grow up quickly, as did all my brothers and sisters. I was not able to go through some of the normal stages of childhood and just enjoy being a child. I learned what I knew mostly from my friends, from the street, or by chance. You accepted adult responsibility early in life. I started babysitting for friends when I was seven or eight years old. I used to help care for my next door neighbor's grandson. At home, I was in charge of my nephew Paul since he was little. Paul pretty much had to go with me wherever I went.

You learned to take care of yourself really quickly. If I had to describe my character as a young child, I would say that I was happy, outgoing, idealistic, strong-willed, self-sufficient, naïve, good-natured, and very bold at times. Now, how is that for a description? I very much enjoyed the simple things in life such as the whisper of a warm gentle breeze blowing on a summer evening. Being self-sufficient and strong-willed are typical character traits in all my brothers and sisters. Now, I was by no means a perfect child. I could have a serious attitude; I picked on other children at times, and believe it or not I am a great whiner. I can whine with the best of them.

At the ripe old age of three, I was very independent and pretty much did my own thing. I was physically bigger (chubbier) than other children my age, so I looked (and probably acted) older than I was. Although I probably acted more mature for my age in some respects, I drank a bottle until I was about five years old and sucked my thumb until I was about eleven years old. Mary, a girl my age, who lived down the street from my family, was my regular playmate until my family moved from there. Playing outside was my favorite thing to do. I loved the outdoors and the beauty of the day. Mom told me I was never at home.

One day on one of my adventures in the neighborhood, I ran into an old man and this was not a good thing. This old man took my hand and said he was going to take me to the store and get me some candy. And oh, I was gone, because I wanted some candy. I remember going up the hill to the store. This old man was holding my hand. Before we got to the store, I remember him stopping and urinating on the wall. I turned my head away from what he was doing, and then when he was done we proceeded to the store. The man gave me some money and sent me into the store to buy some candy. The man that was working in the store must have known who I was. He called my mother and told her that I was there, and he must have told her what was going on. The man at the store told me that my mother needed me at home and that I had to go home right then. I was so excited because I thought my mother needed me. Well, what was awaiting me would not be so good. I remember opening the front door excited to be needed by my mother, and much to my surprise I got the beating of my life. I still can remember my mother had a wooden spoon, and one of my sisters held me down while my mother beat me. I crisscrossed my arms across my chest and pulled my knees up to my chest trying to protect myself. I can still hear my mother screaming at me as she beat me with the spoon saying, "Men are no good."

Associating and hanging out with older people was typical for me. I recall two teenage girls, Nan and Julie, who lived a couple of houses down from our house. Going to their house was the highlight of my day, because Nan and Julie had a vanity in their bedroom. They would let me sit at their vanity and put on make-up. For those of you who are older, do you remember the small sample lipsticks that Avon would give you with a purchase of its products? Well, I just thought they were so cute and probably thought they were made just for me. Of course, Nan and Julie had lots of lipstick samples, and I loved putting them on. And from those vanity visits to their house was born a dream to someday be an actress or even Ms. America. I even remember telling my favorite uncle one day that I was going to Hollywood, and he just laughed. I thought I was definitely Hollywood bound. Not!

Running away from home was something my mother says I did a lot. One day, my mom said that she and my dad were ready to go to work, and they had no idea where I was. So, they went looking for me and could not find me. My mother said that all of a sudden from around the corner, I came walking with my dog on a leash and several other dogs walking right beside and behind me. She told me that she wished she had a camera that day. I'm sure it was a picture she would have loved to capture on film. I can still recall that memory, and yes, I think it was a perfect Kodak moment.

There are probably a quite a few more runaway stories I could tell you, but I'll leave it at that.

My academic career did not get off to a good start. I was three years old when I started kindergarten, but would soon turn four. Now, my kindergarten experience was unique and a fine example of my need to express my independence. School was not a place I wanted to be. Dad worked second shift and was home during the day. I wanted to stay home with my dad. One reason I wanted to stay home was that my dad would go grocery shopping during the day, and I wanted to go with him. I thought I would be missing out on something if I didn't go with him. The second reason I wanted to stay home was that I didn't like school or the teacher.

At this time in my life, my family lived in a different city, which I'll call Glenwood. We only lived there approximately six months. Now, I was attending kindergarten, but not without a fight. I remember my family and a neighbor trying to bribe me to go to school. One day the lady across the street even offered to let me wear her pearl necklace if I would go to school, but that didn't work. One day my oldest sister Jean offered to take me to school. Jean was old enough to drive, so she drove me to school. I can still see her two-door, brown Eldorado with a cream colored, landau roof pulling up in front of the school to drop me off. Before I got out of her car, I told her to wait right there for me 'cause I would be right back. So, I got out of the car and went into school by myself, walked down to my classroom, and went straight to the teacher's desk. I remember telling the teacher that if she was ever going to be mean to me again, let me know now because I was going to leave. On that note, I left the school building and headed for home. I'm sure the teacher called my mom. My mother said she did not know what the teacher did to me for me to say and do what I did. Throughout my life, I usually didn't have a problem telling people just the way it was, but not in a scornful way. And yes, I was a kindergarten drop-out, but that teacher had to be awfully mean for me to be so bold. When I was growing up, going to or completing kindergarten was not requirement. Soon, my family returned to the city just outside of Pittsburgh. This is where I lived most of my life.

In spite of my downfall in my early academic career, I did make it to first grade. I attended a Catholic school for eight years. My teacher was a nun named Sister Agatha. She taught me in both first and second grade. Sister Agatha loved me. I probably still had that "adorable thing" going on, and I found favor with her. This was a good thing considering my traumatic kindergarten experience. Anyway, Sister Agatha would always give our class a snack in the afternoon. Because I was her favorite, I always got extra snacks and special privileges.

I recall one special privilege Sister Agatha gave me. In second grade, you were able to make you First Holy Communion. Making your communion was a very special occasion our school commemorated. Two or three first grade girls were chosen to be what the nuns called "angels." Being an "angel," meant that you participated in the communion ceremony. And you probably guessed it; I was chosen to be one of those "angels." You were required to wear a yellow dress for the communion ceremony. My mother bought me a beautiful yellow dress. In that dress, I thought I was the most beautiful girl there. The communion ceremony was held at Sunday morning mass and my favorite uncle, Tom, was in attendance. I couldn't wait to talk to him and ask him if he saw me walking down the aisle in my yellow dress. Uncle Tom came to our house after mass that day. He had a camera and I insisted that he take a picture of me in my dress. I remember spreading out the dress like it had wings and twirling around so my uncle could take my picture. Being an "angel" and wearing that beautiful yellow dress made me feel just like one.

In first grade you started to learn your prayers (i.e. Our Father/Hail Mary) and were taught Catholic doctrine in catechism class. Catechism classes were part of the Catholic curriculum. Our religion proclaimed belief in the Trinity: God the Father, God the Son, and God the Holy Spirit, and so this made my prayer time a little bit of a challenge. My comprehension and perception of the Trinity concept was probably not quite clear to me. When I prayed, I prayed to all three persons of the Trinity individually. Praying to all those people took what seemed like an eternity to me. I prayed consistently and frequently, but one day while I was praying by myself I recall getting aggravated, because I thought it was taking me too long. I recall stopping in the middle of my prayer and out loud (I usually prayed out loud) I said, if you are all the same people then I'm just praying to one of you, "God." I probably chose God, because he was the common denominator or perhaps the first person mentioned, and my prayer time was never again the same. Since I was only in first grade, I guess I just didn't grasp the concept of the Trinity.

My dad was a praying man. Every morning he would get out his prayer book, sit down at the dining room table and say his prayers. Prayer time was observed regularly at meals and at bedtime in our house. When Dad came home from work he would end his day by praying over all of us and blessing us while we were sleeping. Then he would do a body count to make sure all the kids were accounted for. At times, I would wake up and see Dad praying over us, but I don't believe he knew I had seen him. I believe that God heard his prayers for us.

Being the people-pleasing person I was, I usually tried to do everything I was told to do. I never wanted anyone to be mad at me, especially God. I was faithful in attending church, abiding by Catholic ordinances to the best of my ability and doing what I thought God required of me. If Dad told me to go and pray, I did! One night, dad told me to go and pray and off I went. I remember kneeling in front of the dresser in my parents' bedroom and praying. On the dresser was a statue of the Blessed Mother Mary and baby Jesus. I prayed to and kissed the baby quite often. Oh, how I loved that baby. Somehow, I knew that baby was very special. After a while, Dad came to check on me. He sneaked halfway up the stairs to the landing. Dad peeked around the corner and saw me praying. I could see him out of the corner of my eye, but I don't think he knew I had seen him. I continued to pray and I can still see the smile on my dad's face as he turned around and quietly made his way back down the steps.

Earlier, I mentioned that you were able to make you First Holy Communion in second grade, but you had to make your first confession first. When you went to confession, you told the priest all your sins and then asked forgiveness. Then he would give you absolution. And you had to say however many Hail Marys and Our Fathers the priest told you to do as part of your repentance. The priest acted as an intercessor between you and God.

In order to receive communion, you had to go to confession at least once a week. My view of what I considered to be sin was very limited. Lying, stealing, disobeying my parents, fighting, missing church and using foul language was "my" basic sin list. Remember, I said that you had to go to confession at least once a week in order to be able to receive communion. According to my sin list, I was running out of sins to confess. In other words, I tried to be good and do everything right. So, this is what I did. Every time I went to confession, I would make up some sins. To complete my confession, I would say my final sin which was, "I lied." Saying I lied would cover everything I just made up. I had some serious tunnel vision about sin. If the priest ever caught on to what I did, he never said anything. Isn't it amazing how quick-witted your mind can be at such a young age?

Growing up, I was very content doing my own thing or being by myself. My own little secluded, illusive world was happy, safe, and somewhat short of reality. For example, I remember playing in one of the bedrooms. I would take my sister Charity's Barbie Doll and play in the dresser drawer. Back then the dresser drawers were very wide and deep. You could literally fit your whole body in the drawer with no problem. Anyway, I would put on Barbie's blue high-heel shoes, my favorite shoes for her, and sing my favorite song, "Downtown." Feeling so safe in my own little world, I would just sing and dance the Barbie around in the drawer. I would always keep watch to make sure no one saw me. Although I played with my brothers and sisters, I didn't feel close to them. I always felt I was different. For instance the birth order in our family, it was girl-boy all the way down until it came to me. Then it was my sister and me, then boy and girl. I thought I should have been a boy and wondered why God did not let me be a boy. I didn't have a lot of friends, although I knew a lot of people. I was a tomboy, tough and strong, and somewhat of a loner. I liked playing with the boys. They were my buddies. When I was about eight years old, I had what I considered to be my first best friend. Her name was Sarah. She lived across the street from my family. We were inseparable for a few years. I was what I would call a one-friend-at-a-time person, a devoted friend, because I would give my all to that person to maintain our friendship.

At the age of nine, I got an early start in the work force by delivering the morning paper. A girl delivering newspapers was not a common thing when I was growing up. Being the tomboy I was, I thought that whatever the boys could do so could I. And so, I set out to prove I was just as good as the boys. I delivered the *Pittsburgh Post-Gazette* six days a week by myself, but my dog Rags almost always came with me. I did not have someone to drive me door to door. Whatever the weather conditions were, I still had to deliver the papers. I was a dedicated and responsible worker. Sometimes, I would deliver the papers as early as 2:00 a.m., except for Saturdays. Saturday was what I considered my day off. I could sleep late, and it was payday for my dog and me. If you know anything about delivering the morning paper you know that people want their paper early. My customers would not even think about calling and complaining. This is where my strong will would kick in; you see; I had them trained. For example, one time my paper route manager, John, told me that a customer called and complained that I didn't put the paper in the mail box. I told John that the customer never asked me to put the paper in the mail box. I told him that the next time this person has a complaint to tell me, not him. I do not believe I ever heard another complaint from my manager after that. Now, payday meant stopping at the corner store to get snacks for me and fifty cents worth of Jumbo for my dog Rags. When I was growing up, you could get a lot of Jumbo for fifty cents. Oh, Rags liked the snacks too.

Some time later, my mother said to me that the man who owned and operated the corner store told her that I would buy Jumbo for Rags. I thought she was mad at me so I told her that I bought Rags fifty cents worth of Jumbo because he had to get paid for coming with me all the time. I considered myself a fair person. So, I thought Rags deserved to be paid for his work in protecting me. I didn't even know that the man at the store knew my mother, let alone talked to her. But you know what? God had all kinds of people watching over me.

From my perception, my family was very emotionally distant and remote. You had a sense of understanding that they cared about you and loved you, but my family usually did not express these emotions verbally. You had to be tough like a steel rod and no one could ever know you weren't tough. Words like "I love you," were not usually spoken in our house. My dad did not express himself emotionally and did not say he loved you, but it was understood. I felt my mother's love was conditional, meaning that if you were good and did what she wanted you to do, then you were loved for the time being. I learned to find my self-worth and identity through the approval of others by being a people pleaser.

Sex was a bad word, and your sexuality was not something you talked about in our home and something you did not acknowledge. For example, as a young girl my mother never told me about menstruation. It just happened. You didn't acknowledge the changes that were happening to you and you never talked about it. The messages I received were that sex and sexuality were a dirty secret and something to be ashamed of. Also, when I was a little girl my dad forbid us to parade around the house in our pajamas. Pajamas were just for sleeping in at night. When you awoke from sleeping, you were expected to put on regular clothes. If you came downstairs with your pajamas on my dad would send you right back upstairs to put on you regular clothes.

Anger was a prominent emotion in my family. It was often displayed in our home. For instance, at times when my mother was angry she would go into a rage. Sometimes, during her rage, I would watch my mom hurt herself by banging her head against the wall as she cried and screamed at the top of her lungs. Just like a tornado, my mom would knock over, throw, break, and destroy anything that was in her pathway. One day, when my mom came home from work, and the dishes were not dried and put away, my mother picked up the whole container of dishes and threw them out into the middle of the yard. Another time, my mom and dad and some of my brothers and sisters were watching a Disney movie on television. My sisters Susan, Hope, and I were supposed to be drying the dinner dishes during commercials. Well, Susan and Hope did not really want to dry the dishes, so I told them I would dry them. My mother went into one of her rages when she came into the kitchen and saw that I was the only one drying the dishes. As she was screaming and yelling she threw all the clean pots, pans, and dishes all over the kitchen floor. All the pots, pans, and dishes had to be washed again. As a result of this, some of my brothers, sisters, and I lashed out at each other in the same ways. There were many more anger explosions in our home and throughout my life.

Verbal abuse became normal to me. Being screamed and yelled at just about daily were normal. The things you were asked to do and did, never seemed to be good enough or perfect enough. After being told so often that the things you did weren't good enough, you received the message that you're not good enough. I suffered through emotional abuse by the withholding of love and approval. Also, my mom liked to play mind games with us. She would tell you one story and tell someone else a different story, just to see what you would do. She wanted to see whose button she could push first and who would do what she wanted first.

The physical abuse was a pain I felt I could endure. When I was growing up, upright vacuum cleaners were not invented yet. Your vacuum cleaner was a canister with attachments that you could connect to make the vacuum arm stand upright. So, one time two of my sisters and my youngest brother and I took our baths and got ready for bed. One at a time we were told to go upstairs. Then as we started toward the steps, one of my older family members took the aluminum attachment from the vacuum and started swinging at us. We had to make a run up the steps as fast as we could. The aluminum attachment really stung. I had to cry to make this person stop hitting me, but then when I got to the top of the steps, I would burst out laughing. I remember my little sister crying. She would get angry with me, because I was laughing. You ended up having welts and black and blue marks on you from being hit. At this particular time, I do not know what the reason for this punishment was. It appears to me now that the punishment usually came way after the fact of whatever it was that you did wrong. At some other times, a different family member used to hit us with the two-by-fours that were used back then to go across the frame on the bed to hold the box spring and mattress on. There were many other times like this. Later in my life, my mom told me that when she found out we were being hit, she said she put a stop to it. When I talked to one of my family members regarding the beatings, this person said that they didn't know at the time that this was wrong, because this person used to get hit by another older family member also.

The rage in some members of my family was intense at times. I was terrified of my family's anger. It was a fight for survival of the fittest and a power struggle for control. My father used to always say, "We had a lot of chiefs, but not enough Indians." As for myself, I feel I was more of an Indian. I was usually compliant and I tried to be a peacemaker. Due to my family's anger and rage, the fear that became mine was extreme. At the sound of loud voices, I would become startled. I became overly sensitive to loud voices and extremely responsive to escalating anger in general. Just like an antenna scanning for a signal to tune into, my antenna had to be able to scan and detect people's anger before it exploded. When their anger would explode or if I would detect that anger, then I would disappear in order to protect myself. My need to be perfect, do everything right, and be good was something I strived to achieve. I thought being perfect would prevent the screaming and yelling, but I was wrong.

I was a very emotional child and lived in an emotional battlefield. I cried a lot. But while I was growing up, some people considered me a happy-go-lucky person. My emotions were like riding a roller coaster, up and down, and usually to the extreme, either happy or sad. I could not find a balance with my emotions. Emotionally, I had to always be on my guard. I was becoming an emotional eater, and what I would consider a closet eater. I recall one time my sister Jean took me and a couple of the other kids to eat at a restaurant. I remember eating all my food, the food that the other kids didn't eat, and I asked Jean to buy me more food. I had many more times like this one. As I got older, you would probably never guess that I ate or could eat so much, because I learned to eat in secret. I could go all day without eating and then I would binge at night, when I was alone. At night, I would sometimes buy the largest bag of potato chips, a couple of pints of ice tea, candy, or some other type of junk food, and a big bowl of ice cream and go to my bedroom and eat everything. I never wanted anyone to see what I ate and how much. I actually felt and sometimes still feel ashamed to eat in front of other people. Needless to say, I was very self-conscious of my weight and body size. I remember some relatives commenting about my weight. One time one of my aunts was going to take me to a park. If I remember correctly, I was about four years old. I went to her house dressed in what I thought was a cute, little, blue, polka-dot sun outfit. When I got to my aunt's house, we were standing on her porch, and she told me that I was too fat to wear the outfit I had on. And I thought I looked cute. Throughout my childhood, there were other relatives that commented on my weight and not in a positive manner. However, at a young age, maybe eight or nine years of age, I began experimenting with appetite suppressants. I remember my mom had a box of different flavored appetite suppressants that looked like caramels. So, I sneaked quite a few of them to try. They tasted just like candy. I wanted to see if the suppressants would work, but they didn't. I don't even think I knew exactly what the suppressants were supposed to do. Throughout my life, I have tried other diet remedies such as Weight Watchers and an over-the-counter appetite suppressant, Dexedrine. I only tried Dexedrine, but I didn't like the effect it had on me, so I threw it away. On my last encounter in my early twenties with a quick, weight-loss remedy, I joined a weight program similar to Jenny Craig. You had to eat certain foods for a number of days and so on. I paid one-hundred-fifty dollars to join, in an attempt to finally conquer my weight problem. After the first week, I came to the realization that I was not going to eat like that for the rest of my life, so I quit. It was a wise decision to quit, but I lost all of my money. Throughout my life, I had joined a number of fitness programs or spas, and just about bought every piece of exercise equipment on the market. My sister Charity, used to call my exercise equipment, clothes hangers. She was right. That was just what they were. I would pile all my clothes on them, and never use them. Maybe, my weight problem became a safety net for me. I learned to deal with all my insecurities and fears by eating food to comfort me.

Our family's relationship with dad's family deeply affected my life at a young age. The story as I know it is that some members of my dad's family didn't like my mom. My grandfather and some of my dad's family lived right around the corner from our house. When I was about seven years old, a situation occurred in which the court ordered our family to sever all relations with my dad's family. This meant that our family was not allowed to visit or talk to my grandfather or any other of my dad's relatives. I can remember my mother standing in our kitchen telling me I could no longer talk to or visit my grandfather and my favorite uncle again. I loved to visit and talk to my grandfather and uncle, and they were taken away from me. That day I overheard my mom telling someone in the kitchen that day that she felt the court decision would affect me the most. I remember feeling like I was not good enough for them. At that time, I recall thinking to myself that this court decision will be my dad's family's loss, but none the less I'm sure I felt a sense of rejection. As the years went by eventually we were able to visit my dad's family again, but the conflict between my dad's family and my mom has never ended.

My relationship with my mother was very strained. I did not feel I could trust my mother. I feel that I never bonded with her, and she was not able to nurture me like a mother should. I feel that my mother favored the boys in the family. Maybe that's why I thought I should be a boy. One time I recall my sister Susan saying that my mother raised sons, not daughters. Maybe I thought if I were a boy, my mom would love me more. I remember that I always wanted to be with my mother, but it seemed like she was never there for me. My mother worked a lot. Thinking back on my younger years, I feel that I received a sense of my mom's rejection at an early age. When I was about three years old, our dog bit me on my arm because I took his bone away from him, after my dad told me not to do that. I had to go to the hospital. I remember my mom yelling in anger and rage at my dad, telling him that he had to take me to the hospital, because she wasn't. In fear, I remember crawling under the kitchen table and clinging to the leg of the table. I do not believe that my mother's anger was directed toward me. However, through the eyes of a child it said to me that I was an imposition to her. There were many other times I felt that I imposed on my mother. The message that I received was that she did not want to be bothered with me. Therefore, as I grew older I never wanted to impose on anyone, and I learned very well how to detect if I was imposing on someone. As time went on and my mother was not there for me for whatever reason, the message was reinforced to me and I stopped wanting her.

Growing up, I felt like my mother was never interested in me. Our conversations were usually centered on someone else or what someone was or wasn't doing to her. Looking back, I searched for a mother a good part of my life. When I was a child, I was not consciously aware that I was seeking a mother. For example, in high school, I was close with our secretary, Mrs. B. I don't know why, but one day I started calling her mom, probably just for fun. She was okay with my calling her that. The name caught on and soon I was not the only one calling her mom. Also, there were a couple of teachers that I probably saw as mother figures. Later, when I finished high school I believe my search for a mother continued. I did not feel that my mother could ever be happy for me. For instance, when I was nineteen years old my friend Sandy and I planned a ten day trip to California. My mom wanted to go with us, but what teenager wants her parents to go on a trip with her. Anyway, the morning I was leaving for my trip I went to tell her goodbye. My mom was asleep on the couch. I called to her again and there was no response. At the time, I tried to tell her good-bye, but she wouldn't wake up or acknowledge me. It appeared to me that my mother was mad, because I was going on a trip and she wasn't going with me. As I look back, my mother was mad, but what she was actually doing was giving me the "silent treatment." The "silent treatment" was something my mother did often, to prove her point or manipulate someone to get what she wanted. As I got older and other situations came up, I came to the realization that my mom knowingly did not choose to respond to me.

Always, I desired my mother's love and acceptance. If my mother only knew how much I wanted to be her best friend! As time went on, I knew that I could never have the mother/daughter relationship I desired, wanted, and felt I needed.

I feel that my relationship with my father was good. I felt he understood me and I could trust him. I spent a lot more time with him. I felt that my father was interested in me and what was going on in my life. He was not critical, but accepting. I felt like I could tell my dad anything, although he used to tell me that I talked too much.

As a young child, my perception of my parents' relationship was that it was strained and troubled. For example, one time or even a couple of times, my mother would tell me how she would have to call my dad at work and "make an appointment" with him to have sex. This was information I did not need to know. Often, my sisters and I would attend family functions with my dad taking my mother's place, because she did not want to go with him. My mother expressed to me many times that she did not like being alone with my dad. When I was still young, my parents no longer shared a room. The couch became my mother's bedroom for as long as I can remember.

As I mentioned earlier, my dad did not say much about anything. My mother's anger was something I felt I had to protect my dad from. From a child's point of view, I guess I felt that my dad was not aware of how violent my mom's anger could be, but I knew. I thought I was invincible, a mighty warrior who was strong enough to take on the world. One time, I was getting ready to go out the door and visit my friend Sarah. My mother got angry with me for wanting to leave the house, and she said I never stayed at home. She did not want me to leave, because she would be home alone with my dad. I thought I was their intercessor and would often feel guilty if I left the house. I know at times my dad would do ornery things to irritate my mom, but nothing that was violent. Although, I never witnessed physical violence between my parents, I felt extremely responsible for their well-being. I felt like I was the parent. What did I think I protected my parents from? That was a good question. As a young child, maybe I thought I protected my parents from having to communicate or confront one another to keep the peace or keep them safe. Or, was it my own fear of the anger and rage I had seen all my life? The many different things I had gone through and experienced were shaping my life and the person I was becoming.

As I think back to my childhood, I can think of a specific time in which fear was created in me and is still a part of my life. My mother told me quite a few times when I was growing up that she was going to run away, and not tell anyone where she was going, and never come back. My throat would close up, and the terror and fear that came upon me was beyond words. I was always terrified she would leave. In later years, I found out she also told some of the other kids the same thing. My mom was also always dying. She would often say, "When I die." I don't think she ever told me why she thought she was dying or if there was any just cause of what she thought was the reason was, but she was dying or running away. My mother had many health problems, but I didn't think she would die from them. Thus, the fear of abandonment was born in me. As I grew older, I became afraid that everyone would leave me as well. So, I did not allow myself to get close to people and form serious relationships, because it was safer for me. Eventually, I became a prisoner to my own fears and insecurities. To this day allowing people, including God, to get close to me continues to be a challenge for me.

My perception of the world at this time in my life was that it was "mean." I felt like I had no one I could truly depend on. I recall one beautiful sunny morning as I was on my way to deliver the morning papers. I was about eleven years old. I began to pray. My prayer went something like this: Dear God, I think I just want to live to be about twenty years old. Yes, I think that will be long enough, because everybody is so mean. I do not know why I picked twenty years old to want to die, but I can only guess that twenty years old must have seemed ancient to me. I do not recall what was going on in my life at this time to warrant such strong feelings. Actually, at the age of twenty I did seriously consider taking my life. I remember that I wanted to drive my car off a bridge that was close to where I lived. But then I thought about my favorite movie, *It's a Wonderful Life,* the part where George Bailey (a character in the movie) wanted to take his life by jumping off the bridge, but an angel stopped him and showed him what life would have been like without him. And I thought about the many people I would hurt by taking my life, including God. Also, I decided that I did not want to be someone's statistic, but little did I know I was already a statistic. Suicidal thoughts became prominent throughout my life. I never attempted suicide, but I did seriously consider it a couple of times. As time went on, I always felt like there was something wrong with me inside, but I still did not know what.

Chapter 3

My Big Adventure
(The Rebellious Years)

"Remember not the sins of my youth and my rebellious ways: according to your love remember me, for you are good, O Lord." Psalm 25:7

Victory, Victory let's repeat it...Never will we be defeated...

Finally, no more Catholic School, eight years was enough. Now that was something to cheer about, or so I thought. My parents planned for me to go to a Catholic High School, but they changed their mind. I went to a public high school all four years of high school. On the first day of my ninth year of school, my mother told me to go to the public high school and register. So, I registered myself into ninth grade. In rebellion, I decided that I wasn't going to use my given name of Elizabeth; instead, I used my nickname Betsy.

My attitude became more defensive and bold, and my spirit was becoming more rebellious. No one was going to tell me what I could and could not do. In high school I guess I had somewhat of a negative outlook on life. One of my teachers with whom I felt close once commented to me that I was very pessimistic. I had no idea what pessimistic meant, and I do not know what I said that prompted her comment. My teacher explained to me what pessimistic meant. At that time, I am not sure I grasped the concept of being pessimistic, but as I reflect on those days I agree with her comment. Back then, if you had asked me where I saw myself five years from then; most likely I would tell you I did not know, because I could not see past today. I would usually anticipate the worst. If something were going to go wrong, it would happen to me. I felt nothing good could or would ever happen to me. Setting goals or making plans for the future was something I did not do. The words "I can't" were a frequent part of my everyday vocabulary. I could explain my pessimism with an old psychology concept. The concept is the half-full/half-empty experiment. You take a half cup of water and then determine whether the cup is half-full or half-empty. If you say that the cup is half-full then you would be considered an optimistic person. If you say that the cup is half-empty then you would be considered a pessimistic person. I have always seen the cup as half-empty. Since those good old high school days, I have taught myself to say that the cup is half-full, and I believe more now that good things can happen to me.

God was no longer as important to me, and I began to drift away from Him. Now, I had my own agenda. I no longer cared if I attended church regularly, which used to be very important to me. Six days a week plus of going to church in Catholic School was enough for me. So, on some Sundays my friend Sarah and I would make an appearance in church and either stand in the back lobby or sit in the basement for a short period of time. My appearance in church was just to say that I was there. Sarah's boyfriend at the time drove a van. So, we would leave church and go driving around with him. One day, I tried to justify my not going to church as much and relieve my guilt by saying to myself something to the effect of, "God doesn't do anything for me anyway, so why should I go to church." Well, I'm sure God was not happy with me on that day. Now, I believe that my saying that was a slap in the face to God.

Anyway, I made some new friends in school and joined a sorority. Sarah and I remained friends, but we were not as close and did not hang out like we used to. I liked going to high school, because I loved the people, unlike my kindergarten experience. I remember one time, one of the assistant principals, Mr. James, came to me and said; Ms. Lane do you know what I like best about you?"

And I said, "My eyes," because a lot of people liked my eyes; I guess because they were different, and some people said they were pretty.

Anyway, Mr. James said, "No, I like your "insight." Well, you know that word was not in my vocabulary.

So, I said to him, "What is that?" Mr. James explained the meaning of the word to me and why he liked my insight. It was a great compliment. The Lord was already showing me some gifts I had.

I started using curse words a lot. There was an old saying about cussing like the sailors. In time, I became a pro at it and probably could cuss better than the sailors. My perception of cussing was that it meant you were grown-up. Although I was not a behavior problem in school, I had a few minor incidences, but nothing serious. I was tough and would speak my mind. For example, my Algebra I class in ninth grade was a real challenge. I did not like the teacher, because he was mean, and I didn't think he taught us like he should have. And I did not learn anything in his class. I remember at the end of the school year, he saw me in the hall and told me that I was failing. I recall getting smart with him, telling him that I didn't like him and that I didn't care if

I failed the class. So, I had to retake Algebra I in tenth grade. I got an "A" the second time I took Algebra I. One day, I saw the Algebra I teacher that I had in ninth grade at my school. I went up to him and told him that I was getting an "A" in algebra. He said that was because he was a good teacher. I got smart with him and told him he was not a good teacher. I told him I was getting an "A" because the teacher I had now was a good teacher. If I were in school today, this definitely would have been an office referral. Academically, I would consider myself an average student, but I could have done better if I had really applied myself.

I experienced the repercussions of cheating. When I was in the tenth grade I was on my way to my English class to take a test. A friend of mine passed me in the hallway and gave me what I thought was a note, so I took it. It turned out to be a cheat sheet. This was an unplanned thing, because I didn't realize it was a cheat sheet until later. Anyway, I was not good at these things. I usually always got caught if I was doing something wrong. Well, I sat in the first row in English class and sure enough I got caught cheating and got a zero for the test. I think that was the last time I took a cheat sheet to class.

I considered myself to be somewhat athletic. I loved to play sports. When I was younger I wanted to play baseball with the boys, but back then girls were not permitted to play baseball. Again, I just wanted to prove I was just as good as the boys. In ninth grade I signed up to play softball. I played all four years of high school. I pretty much rode the bench in ninth grade, but I had so much fun. Eventually, I did get to play more. Some of the positions I played were pitcher, catcher, and first base. One of the referees used to call me "twinkle toes," because he said I did not keep my foot on the base when I played on defense. The highlight of playing softball in high school was winning second place in our division when I was in eleventh grade.

Against all odds, in the spring of tenth grade I tried out for cheerleader. You see, I was not your stereotypical cheerleader. I was not skinny, but overweight. People would irritate me, because I felt that some people didn't think overweight people could do anything, but they were wrong. So, I set out to prove a point and tried out for the cheerleading squad. I wanted to show people that even though I was overweight, I could cheer and do stunts just as well as the other girls. I remember sitting in my homeroom on the day that the principal was announcing over the loudspeaker the tryout numbers of the girls who made it for the cheerleading squad. I was so excited. I told my homeroom teacher that the principal was going to announce my number over the loudspeaker. I remember my homeroom teacher laughed and commented saying that I was not going to make the squad. My intention was to quit right after I made the squad, because I had only wanted to prove a point. But, I ended up not quitting the squad, because I loved it and felt I was good at it. I cheered for my last two years in high school. I love defying the odds and doing things some people thought I could not do.

Back when I was in high school, football and basketball games were well attended with crowds of sometimes over a couple hundred. Due to my being overweight, I endured a lot of public humiliation, during my cheerleading days. While I would be cheering, I could hear people calling me names, pointing me out, making fun of me, and saying how fat I was. One time, when I was on the football field cheering, I recall some girl yelling down from the bleachers at me saying, "Look at that girl with the big thighs kick her legs." The ridicule I endured only reinforced my belief that I was not good enough. But somehow, I had the strength to go on in spite of being made fun of, and I cheered on.

My stepping out to prove that I could be a cheerleader, in spite of being overweight, proved to be a good thing. In my senior year of high school, a young lady who was a little overweight (or what other people thought was over-weight) approached me and told me she was going to try out for cheerleader. She said she was trying out because I did it and she felt it was okay. My point was well taken and I had encouraged someone else to beat the odds. Also, it broke the cheerleader stereotype in our school. By the way, the young lady did make it on the cheerleading squad. In spite of the public ridicule, cheering and playing softball in high school were the best things I did for myself and the highlight of my high school days.

I met a girl named Sandy in my first year of high school. We did not pursue a friendship at this time, but Sandy would later become my best friend. Sandy was a cheerleader, adventurous, a risk taker, and one of the most popular girls in school. I was not adventurous or popular, nor did I take risks. When I made the cheerleading squad, Sandy and I had a mutual agreement; she hated me and I hated her. However, during the summer before our junior year we became best friends. There were a lot of good things that came out of our friendship. Sandy had been driving since she was about twelve years old, even though she didn't have a license. The day she turned sixteen years old, Sandy went and got her driver's license. I did not really have an interest in learning to drive. Sandy said that I had to get my license, because everybody did. She said if I got my driver's license, then we would have more cars to use between her family and mine. It took some time, but Sandy finally convinced me to get my license. In the spring of my sixteenth year, I got my driver's license. If it were not for Sandy, I do not think I would have ever pursued the opportunity to learn how to drive. I do thank God that I learned to drive. Although I did not agree with all the adventures that Sandy wanted to venture after, I feel that I was given the opportunity to do some things that I might have never had the opportunity to experience otherwise.

For Sandy, there were no limits and nothing was out of her reach. We had some really great times in high school and it truly was "my big adventure." However, we sometimes placed ourselves in situations that were dangerous. For example, we would take walks around what we called the "big block." This walk took approximately two to three hours. We usually walked late at night. When we were growing up, this seemed pretty safe. Nonetheless, there were times when strangers stopped and tried to pick us up. One time, some people in a car chased us and tried to run us over. This was a very scary thing, but it didn't stop us. There was another incident involving Sandy, our friend Trish, and me. On our "big block" walk we stopped to talk to some boys. We did not know the boys. I did not really engage myself in the conversation with these guys. They wanted us to go for a ride in their van. I did not want to go. What I said next, they would not let me forget. I was scared and I told Sandy that those boys could rape us. Well, Sandy and Trish laughed hysterically. I did not know why I felt the way I did or what prompted me to say what I said, but I did. The fear that embraced me was an unusual response to that situation. Sandy and Trish gave me some money to take the bus home. I left, and Sandy and Trish went with the boys. I walked to the bus stop to catch the bus. I was so scared that I hid on someone's steps until the bus came. Fortunately, we all made it home safely.

Engaging in conversations with people I did not know was not something I did often, but I was not aware of it. My friend Sandy pointed this behavior out to me. One night, Sandy and I were at a bar. Sandy seemed to engage in conversations with other people more easily. So, a couple of guys came over to talk to us. Sandy talked and I listened becoming very quiet. The guys got up and left our table. Then, Sandy said to me, "How come you stop talking when people come over to talk to us?" I remember telling her that I did not know those guys, and I did not have anything to say. Just recently, Sandy told me that back then she had to work harder to engage me in conversations with people, because I would withdraw. She was right. Sometimes, even now, I tend not to engage myself in conversations with people I do not know. Maybe this behavior that tends to draw me away is due to my own insecurities and fears that I am not good enough.

When I was sixteen years old, I tasted my first alcoholic beverage. I was with some friends outside of school and had a half glass of wine. If I recall correctly, I was drinking Boone's Farm Strawberry Hill wine. I didn't take another drink until I was about seventeen years old. I drank occasionally. Then, I began to binge drink, usually on weekends after I graduated from high school. When I drank with my friends, we placed ourselves in danger by drinking and driving. I recall one time I had gone to the bar with Sandy, and we got seriously drunk. We then left and headed for the movie theater. We got behind someone that was not moving fast enough for us, and we wanted to get to the theater before the movie started. So, Sandy kept going faster and ended up within about an inch from his bumper. I told her to stop and let me drive, but she would not stop riding the guy's bumper, and he kept making sudden stops. Sandy and I made it safely to the theater, but when we got into the movie she got sick and we had to go home. Sandy finally agreed to let me drive. We could have had a serious accident while under the influence of alcohol. I thank God that my drinking days were short lived. On my twenty-first (legal age to drink alcohol) birthday, I do not recall having an alcoholic beverage at all. When I drank, I usually got sick and vomited. I consider my drinking days a waste of time and a waste of life. Eventually, probably a few years or so after my twenty-first birthday, I quit drinking altogether. I never engaged in drug use, nor did I ever have the desire to try drugs. When I was growing up, marijuana was one of the drugs of choice. I had quite a few friends who participated in drug use. However, my friends that used drugs never offered them to me, and they would protect me from anyone asking me to participate in drug use. At lunchtime, one day when I was in high school, a group of my friends and I were standing around in a circle, and they were passing a joint around. When the joint got to me, a friend of mine that was standing next to me made a motion to the effect that I didn't smoke pot, and they never bothered me or questioned me. I guess you could say that people just knew not to offer drugs to me. Prior to my first alcoholic drink, my friends and family members who drank never offered me any alcohol either. One day when I was older, my sister Gracie told me that my family did not ask me to go to a bar, because one, I wouldn't go, and two, she said that I didn't belong there. I believe that God protected and guarded me from the desire for alcohol and drugs. With a family history of alcoholics and drug users, the odds were certainly against me. I thank God that He did not allow drugs and alcohol to define me.

Life continued on and our traveling adventures began. When we graduated from high school, Sandy, Trish, and I went to Florida for a two-week vacation. My sister Charity lived there and we stayed with her. My sister planned a great itinerary for us, and we had a great time. Spending time on vacation in Florida with my sister Charity would be part of my summer plans. Then, when Sandy and I were nineteen, we had our biggest adventure going across the country to California. We had a travel agency plan a ten-day trip for us. When we arrived in California we went to get the car that we were renting. The car rental gave us a two-door Mustang that had a couple of problems and was not what we were expecting to drive. The key was locked in the car ignition for our whole trip, someone stole the license plate, and the bucket seats were so high that you were unable to see oncoming traffic clearly enough to get onto the freeway. So,

Sandy would drive and I would tell her when to go. Also, I was the police radar. I had to let her know where the police were, because we were usually exceeding the legal speed limit. If you know anything about California driving, you know that driving and getting onto the freeway can be pretty dangerous.

While in California, our taking risks continued, and we gave little thought to danger. Now, Sandy and I were not of legal drinking age. So, she borrowed her sister's driver's license and I borrowed my sister Susan's license so we would be able to go to the bars and drink in California. One night, we had dinner at a place called Bogart's. Sandy met up with a guy named Ollie. Ollie wanted to take Sandy out, but what would I do? Ollie said that he had a cousin named Dory, and he could be my date. Ollie and Dory were of Iranian descent. I told Sandy that I did not think this was a good idea, but we went anyway. The guys picked us up the next night and our adventure began. Ollie and Dory took us to Newport Beach for dinner. We were having a great time and we never stopped laughing. While we were eating dinner, Ollie kept making comments to me about treating Dory "good." I got the distinct feeling that Ollie wanted me to have sex with Dory. So, Sandy and I went to use the restroom, and I told her that I thought that Ollie wanted me to have sex with Dory. Sandy assured me that Ollie didn't want me to have sex with Dory. After dinner, the guys took us back to their apartment. Ollie took Sandy to show her around their apartment and Dory and I were sitting on the couch, kissing. All of a sudden, Sandy came running down the steps and said to me, "Let's go!" We stormed out of Ollie and Dory's apartment on foot. We had no idea where we were or in what direction our hotel was. I asked Sandy what happened, and she said that Ollie made some inappropriate advances toward her. The guys wanted us to have sex with them. I do not know how we found our way back to our hotel, but we made it safely and unharmed.

Ollie called our hotel room later that night to ask us why we left. Sandy told him that she was not going to have sex with him. Ollie said to her that he "thought that that's what you American girls do." Well, wherever he got his information he was definitely misinformed, because these American girls didn't. I said a few choice words to Ollie and hung up on him. The time in California was definitely an adventure and a fine example of life in the fast lane. Sandy and I still cannot believe that our parents allowed us to venture so far away from home unsupervised. Anyway, we had a great time and many more adventures after California.

I considered myself to be streetwise, but there was a side of me that was completely innocent and unaware of things going on around me. I did not understand a lot of things; they seemed to go right over my head. Let me explain. You could not tell me jokes, especially off-colored jokes, because I simply did not get them. This is how bad it was. Sandy knew that I usually did not get jokes. Her father loved to tell jokes. If her father wanted to tell me a joke, she would think about it and then tell him if he could tell me or not, because she usually knew what joke he had in mind. If it was a joke she thought I would not get, then she would tell me the joke in a way she knew I would understand. Personally, I usually never tell jokes. Even today, I tell people not to tell me jokes, because more than likely I will not get them.

In our young adult days, Sandy and I enjoyed going to the movies. We went as much as we could. For Sandy, our movie going was probably a chore. You see, I had a problem comprehending the movie content or getting the hidden meaning of the movie most of the time. Therefore, I usually talked through the whole movie, asking her questions. Some of the things just went right over my head. However, I never felt uncomfortable asking Sandy questions. She never made me feel like an idiot, but accepted me for who I was. Today, Sandy and I are still good friends. When I visit Sandy and her family now and she tells her husband (Sandy's husband is aware of my inability to get some things, especially at the movies.) that we are going to the movies, he asks her why, because he says that I am not going to understand the movie anyway. One day when he said this, I told him that I was older now, and I knew a little more than I used to.

As I grew older, I began to realize that there were a lot of things about life that I did not have a clue about. One day, my little sister Hope, told me about the eye shadow I wore. She said I had to change the basic blue or green (the sixties look) I wore. I wore these two colors with everything. Hope liked the matching thing; I was not concerned if the eye shadow matched what I was wearing. I was not color coordinated, and I wore what I thought looked good on me. Hope taught me how to apply different shades of eye shadow together, using more than one color and shade. Eventually, I learned to be more color coordinated. Sometimes, I felt like Hope knew so much more than I, even though she was younger than I was. On one occasion, when I was about eighteen years old, I had gone to Sandy's house. I was in her mother's room. Sandy's mom gave me some pressed powder make-up. I told her mom thanks, but I honestly had no idea what it was. When I left the room, I had to ask Sandy what the stuff was and what it was used for. I felt like I lived in my own little secluded world and things just passed me by.

I did not date much when I was in high school. I dated my first official boyfriend in ninth grade. His name was Joe. He was a football player and a wrestler. Joe was a nice guy, and he never made any inappropriate advances toward me. About three weeks into dating. Joe kissed me for the first time. It was a quick kiss, but it was nice. However, after he kissed me something happened to me inside and that was the end of our dating. I called Joe on the phone that night and told him I did not want to go with him anymore. The next day at school my friends teased me and asked me if I broke up with

Joe because I didn't like his kiss. It was not Joe or the kiss; it was me. When I would see Joe after we broke up, I had a bad attitude toward him. I acted angry toward him. Let's just put it this way, I was mean to him. He did not do anything wrong to me to deserve my anger or meanness toward him. My strange response to the kiss baffled me, because I could not explain at the time why I responded the way I did.

In high school usually the boys I liked didn't like me. You see, I was overweight. Guys liked the skinny girls and I did not fall into that category. However, some guys and some people thought I was pretty enough, but not skinny enough. In my senior year of high school, I dated a guy named Marty. I really liked Marty. He was a true gentleman. We had some really good times together, but he would always tell other people where he was going to take me before he even asked me. In other words, I was the last to know where we were going and what we were doing and this did not make me happy. We dated for a while and then parted our ways after high school and it was not because he kissed me. As I reflect on our relationship, after we broke up I had a bad attitude toward Marty and I was angry with him, but I had no reason to be. Again, I did not understand my behavior.

A year or so after high school, I had lost some weight. I was not what I considered skinny, but I was thinner and felt thinner than I had been for what I believed was the first time in my life. I want to give you an example of how some guys and some people have viewed me all my life. My friend Sandy ran into Marty at some point around the time I lost weight. Sandy said that Marty told her that if I had lost some weight he would date me, not just date me, but really date me. I guess that meant a serious relationship. Anyway, Marty did ask me out again and I said no, because at that time he couldn't see past my physical body. My philosophy is if you can't see what is in my heart, then you see nothing at all. I'm sure some people may not agree with my philosophy and I know that some did, but quite a few people still see me as Marty did, even today.

I will never forget what my mother said to me at that time when I had lost the weight. She told me how ugly I looked, and that I did not look good thin. I can still see her smirky little grin as she said this to me. This was just another big rejection chiseling away at my already distorted self-image. I did not stay thin for long. It didn't take me long to put the weight back on and then some. The reality was that being thin did not get me the love and approval I thought it would. I still struggle with my weight today.

I delved into the mythical world of astrology and psychics in my later teens and in early adulthood. I had gone to psychics quite a few times. I liked reading the daily astrology predictions in the newspaper, and I bought the monthly astrology predictions' scroll regularly. For me, listening to a physic predict my future gave me hope and something to look forward to. However, I think God had His guardian angels watching out for me. I figured out that some psychics would have things they would say in general and feed off your response. For example, a psychic might say there is this guy; he has dark hair, and you would get all excited thinking she was going to tell you about the man of your dreams. And it would just so happen that there was a guy with dark hair that you liked, but she did not know anything about him. I know God protected me from this evil, and this is how I know. One day, a friend of mine that I worked with at the time wanted me to go to a new psychic that was in town. She had never been to a psychic and I had quit going to them. Anyway, I agreed to go with her on one condition, that condition being that she did not believe anything the person told her. The psychic took me first and began telling me my fortune. The lady psychic kept telling me that God is all around me. She really didn't say anything else. Then, my friend went in to get her fortune told. When we left, my friend told me that this psychic lady told her something to the effect that somehow close to her was very jealous of her and out to get her. The psychic told my friend that in order to break the curse and protect herself, she had to come back and pay a certain amount of money and participate in certain rituals and prayers. I believe my friend was really scared of what might happen if she did not do as the psychic told her. So, I told my friend that what the psychic told her was not true, and she should not go back and do what the psychic said to do. I believe that my friend did go back to the psychic and did everything the lady told her to. However, my friend never confirmed my belief, and she never talked about the psychic to me again. That was the last time I ever went to a psychic and eventually ceased all forms of astrology. It is amazing how two different people can have two different results, but I still believe that God protected me from the evil spirits.

Just a few weeks ago I listened to a sermon that Charles Stanley of In Touch Ministries was giving. I don't recall the exact title of his sermon, but I do remember him making a comment about horoscopes. Charles Stanley said something to the effect of how can someone who doesn't know you tell you about your future. Just think about it, if your astrological sign is "Leo" and you are reading the newspaper with today's horoscope message in it, you and millions of other people are reading the same message. How can it be true for all of you, when whoever wrote this horoscope message doesn't even know anything about you or anyone else? When I engaged in astrology the thought never crossed my mind that everyone is reading the same message. Charles Stanley made a great point. God clearly warns us in His word about the seeking of psychics or other such things. In Deuteronomy 18: 10-12 it says, "...And don't try to use any kind of magic or witchcraft to tell fortunes or to cast spells or to talk with spirits of the dead. The Lord is disgusted with anyone who does these things…" I used to somewhat, if not completely believe some of those horoscope messages. I know that some people cannot start their day without reading the daily astrology message or talking to a psychic. But just remember, the daily astrology message is not personalized just for you, and wherever the information comes from, it cannot predict your future. It is a general statement for everyone.

There is a product out on the market called a TV Guardian. The TV Guardian is a device you hook up to your television to filter out offensive language from your television set. Maybe God put a God guardian on me to filter out things He did not want me to be subjected to or know at this time in my life.

The English language was somewhat of a challenge for me all my life. I was grammatically challenged. English was not my favorite subject in school, but I got good grades. Actually, I hated English class, because all I did from eighth grade through eleventh grade is diagram sentences. I never got the concept of diagramming sentences. Anyway, during my junior year in high school, I began to notice that people thought I talked differently. I did not pronounce my words correctly. Now, I did not have a speech impairment. Let me explain. I used to add and subtract letters of the words I spoke and pronounced some words differently, or what some people thought was differently. The summer of my junior year, I was at cheerleading camp talking to my friends. I said that the clothes we were going to wear looked like "underwears." Now I thought I said it correctly, but my friends starting laughing at me and asked me to repeat what I said. I repeated what I said about the "underwears" and they said I said it wrong. I asked them to say it, and it sounded like the same thing I said. My friends never told me what was wrong with what I said. It was much later in my life that I figured out that it was underwear, not "underwears."

As I got older, I began to observe that more people started commenting on the way I talked. Quite a few people would ask me if I ever lived in the South, and some insisted that I must have lived in the South. My family lived in the north part of Pittsburgh. So, I would tell them that I came from South-North Pittsburgh. I guess my dialect sounded southern to them, but I didn't think that I talked any differently than anyone else where I lived. However, if you live in Pittsburgh you have the privilege of speaking a language all your own. This unique language is called "Pittsburghese."

Pittsburghese is defined in the book *The Tongue-in-Cheek Guide to Pittsburgh* Volume I:

> It's that special language-within-a-language that is unique to Pittsburgh. Oh sure, people in Boston and Brooklyn and Tupelo talk "funny" too. But Pittsburghese is different. Pittsburghese is words that don't seem to exist anywhere else, like grinny (grandmother) and sputzie (I'm not sure what this one means) and redd up (clean up) and yunz (those ones). Pittsburghese is words we think we've heard elsewhere-like dahntahn (downtown) and Ahiya (hi), hosale (wholesale) – but we're just not really sure. And of course, Pittsburghese is those special Pittsburgh-only words like chipped chopped ham, Smiffilled (Smithfield), Robison (Robinson) and Scroll Hill (Squirrel Hill).

If you are a true Pittsburghese-speaking person you are allowed to add and subtract letters from words, shorten them in length, pronounce them differently or what some people think is incorrectly and give words a whole new meaning.

I personally like to create my own definition for words. Let me give you an illustration. In the *Webster's* II *New Riverside Dictionary*, the word cute is defined as delightfully attractive or clever: shrew. My definition of cute is warm and loving. So, if I say you're cute, I am saying that you are warm and loving. The word cute just gives me a warm fuzzy feeling. For the most part, speaking my own unique language was usually acceptable where I came from. I just love being different. I believe my unique language and the way I speak will always be a part of who I am.

My rebellious days were quickly coming to a close as I began to realize my need to have God in my life again.

Chapter 4

Stolen Innocence

"And as for you, you meant evil against me, but God meant
if for good in order to bring about this present result…"
Genesis 50:20

It was a beautiful and peaceful, starry night. The stars lit up the night as they danced around the clear, royal-blue sky as the night stood still. It was a truly perfect night. It was late at night, and the entire world was fast asleep. The streets were deserted and there was not a soul to be found. It was just me and the night. Through the calm, serene night, I spread my arms like wings and I flew all around. So peacefully, I soared through the sky like an eagle through the still night air. And oh, how I could fly! The beauty of the night was so intriguing it comforted my soul. My soul was free to be me. Oh, to live in a world without fear and not be held captive. And then in the dying moments of my soul, I awoke. The scene I described above was just a dream. It was a recurrent dream throughout my childhood. In my dream I lived in a world without fear, no hurt and no pain, but then life removed my innocence. The nightmares did not end. I remember waking up screaming many nights, but I do not recall anyone coming to see why I was screaming. One night my mother heard me, but I remember her telling me to wake up and go back to sleep. She didn't come to check on me. Some of the nightmares were about bugs such as bees and spiders. I remember in the nightmare the spiders would usually be crawling on me. Why the nightmares? There were so many signs along the way, but no one was paying any attention. I remember crying a lot in high school and throughout my life. If you said boo to me, I would cry. One day at the end of my ninth grade year, it must have been the last day of school or close to it, I was sitting on the steps in the hall with a friend and one of my teachers came over to talk to me. I remember I held my knees close to me and was rocking myself like I was in a rocking chair and if I remember correctly, I was crying. Strange behavior? I was overly sensitive. But no one knew the deep, dark secret that was locked within my heart, not even me. Many nights as I lay in my bed immobilized in terror and paralyzed with fear, my eyes would stay focused on the crack at the bottom of the bedroom door, keeping my guard, and patrolling my soul. Often, I would awake from my sleep, just about every hour. The drop of a pin or any noise or sound I heard, would disrupt my sleep. These behaviors were not typical of the average, normal child. However, I would soon learn that my childhood would not be classified as normal.

I could not explain the reason for my behavior, until one day when I was about sixteen years old. I remember that I was fast asleep in my bed. Suddenly, I awakened to the sound of heavy breathing. Terrified, I just laid in my bed. My body was frozen and lifeless, unable to respond to the sound and unable to speak. Finally, from my bed I called out to one of my brothers to ask what the noise was. He said that he had been exercising. Fear embraced my body and I still could not move from my bed. Eventually, I got up the courage to get up and check out the situation. I checked in on my niece, who was sleeping in the next room. Everything seemed to be okay. It was that night that the deep, dark secret that held my soul captive was unlocked within my heart. And the secret that was locked within my heart was a crime that was committed against me. The secret was that I had been raped as a child. My soul would be damaged forever. The sound of the breathing triggered my memory, and I thought it was happening to someone else. The memories of my rapes came flooding back to me just like a dam that had just released the raging water. I felt like a prisoner entrapped in my soul. My mind could not escape the terror of what happened to me. I remember going to school the next day and telling my best friend Sandy about what happened. I was crying and I do not think I was truly aware of what was happening to me, nor was anyone else.

I could recall the rapes so vividly. I remembered two specific times in which I had been raped. The first time I recall being raped was by a neighborhood boy when I was about three years old. My family and I were living in a city that I will call Homewood. I was playing at a neighbor's house across the street from our house. I recall my sister Susan and one other family member being with me. We were on the second floor of the neighbor's house. The neighbor boy that we were playing with was, I guess, about thirteen years old. I do not recall his name. I remember the boy took me by my right hand and started pulling me hurriedly across the wooden floor to the attic door. I can still hear the sound of my black, patent leather shoes hitting the floor tap, tap, tap as I was running across the wooden floor. My sister Susan and the other family member were still with me. I remember the boy told me the he was going to "show me something fun and it would make me feel good." We got to the attic step. Then the boy and I stepped up on the step and then onto the landing floor of the attic. He shut the door behind us. There was a huge pile of clothes lying on the floor. I can still see him picking me up and throwing me on top of the clothes. I could hear Susan pulling on the door knob asking us what we were doing. Thinking back, the boy probably locked the door, because my sister Susan could not get in. I remember the boy kissing me all over. I can still remember the dress I was wearing; it was blue. I remember that the boy pulled my blue dress up and what happened next, I do not remember. The trauma was stored in my memory and locked within my heart. Looking back to that time, I think that my dad might have suspected that something had happened to me at that house. Because one day, I was over that house up in the attic with what I think may have been the grandfather in that family. My dad came up and got me, spanked my bottom and told me I was not allowed to go over there and play anymore. After I learned to drive, I would be driving around by myself and my soul would navigate me back to the house where I was raped. By this time the house had been demolished and it was just an empty lot covered over, just like my soul. When I would drive to the house, I honestly don't know why I wanted to go there or what I was searching for.

The second time I recall being raped, I was maybe four or five years old and I was raped by a family member. My family had moved from Glenwood. We were now living in the house I lived most of my life in. I was asleep in my parents' room on the floor at the bottom of my parents' bed. I recall my dad asleep in bed. It was probably somewhere in the middle of the night. I was awakened by someone pulling down my pants. My body froze in terror and I kept my eyes closed tight so he did not know I was awake, but I could see him out of the bottom slit of my eyes. Then, he began to rape me. I remember some tears coming out of my eyes, but he didn't see them. I turned over and escaped into my world where there was no hurt or pain. I believe he continued to rape me. The next time I remember awakening he was pulling the sheet I was lying on out from underneath me. I can still recall the color of the sheet. It was pink. No one heard him, not even my dad. My dad had probably been drinking. He usually snored very loudly, and it was usually extremely difficult to wake my dad up when he had been drinking. These are the two times I remember being raped. I am not sure if I was raped more than this.

In John 10:10 it says "that the thief comes only to steal and kill and destroy." And the thief that came in the night thinks that no one knows what happened in the darkness, but you can't hide from God. The rapes damaged my life and pierced my soul forever. I was robbed of my innocence. Maybe, my mother was right when she told me "men are no good." My feelings and emotions were suppressed inside of me. I was numb. The shame I felt was not something that I can describe in words, and the shame would never go away. I hated myself even more. Remembering the rapes only added to the distorted self-image and low self-worth I already had. Often times, a victim of sexual abuse becomes promiscuous, but not me. I went the opposite way. Sex or any form of it was not for me, unless I was married. Now, I could explain the terrifying nightmares and the fear that overcame me. I can explain the anger towards the guys I dated. And now, I can explain why I felt like something was wrong with me all my life, because there was.

Shortly after I remembered my rapes, I recall still feeling like there was something wrong with me. I decided that I needed to see a gynecologist. This was my first experience at the gynecologist and I went by myself. I guess I was looking for an explanation or answer for the way I felt. I can still remember that visit and the doctor's name. His name was Dr. George. I did not tell this doctor that I had been raped. After Dr. George examined me he said that there was nothing wrong with me physically, but he told me that I was "so fat that it was a wonder that I even had a period at all." I know that I was overweight, but he made me feel like I weighed about three hundred pounds. I remember Dr. George told me that I had poor metabolism and prescribed some mediation to help speed up my metabolism; I guess so I could lose weight. This was yet another big blow to how I already felt about myself, but this time it was directed toward my sexuality and being a woman. Surely, this was not something you tell a young girl on a first visit to the gynecologist, especially since I was ignorant and ashamed about my womanhood to begin with. This incident did not make me ever want to go back to a gynecologist. I tried the medication he gave me, but ended up throwing it away. I never went back to see Dr. George ever again.

At the time I did not tell my family about the memories and being raped, probably because I didn't trust them, or maybe I didn't think they would believe me either. Earlier, I said I told my friend Sandy, and I told a teacher with whom I felt close, about the rapes. We didn't really talk about it and nothing happened. I do not think they knew what to do for me. Looking back, their response said to me that my being raped was not a big deal. So, that is how I treated it, as no big deal. My mind knew about the rapes, but my heart would not receive it. Just like a tape recorder, my mind replayed the memories of the rapes day after day, over and over again throughout my adulthood. I knew the vivid details of what I remembered of my rapes by heart. As I got older the memories of my rapes had become more consuming. The memories played in my mind twenty-four/seven, but they were still not a big deal. Ignoring the reality of the rapes, I went on with my life. And what they meant for evil, God would soon turn into good.

Chapter 5

Life After High School

No Plans! No Goals!
No Direction!

"To everything there is a season, and a time to every purpose under the heaven...A time to keep silence and a time to speak...Ecclesiastes 3:1, 7b

At first, I wanted to stay in high school, because it was safe, secure, and I was in my comfort zone. School was structured; there were no risks, and I knew what was expected of me, but it was time to graduate. On June 4, 1979, I graduated from high school. I ranked thirty-two out of about one-hundred-fifty-six students in our graduating class. Not bad, but I'm sure I could have done better had I applied myself. One thing I knew for sure after I graduated from high school was that I didn't need a college diploma to prove that I could make it out there in the world. So, going to college was not an option for me. I had a whole world to prove to that I could make it and that I was good enough. In high school, my perception of the school counselor was that they really didn't pay too much attention to the average student. You had to either be the bad student, failing academically, or the "A" student and college material. I do not ever recall sitting down with the guidance counselor discussing my future and what I would do after graduation. As a matter of fact, I recall talking to the school counselor maybe a couple of times during my high school career, if even that. At one time, I told my dad I wanted to be a lawyer, but then I changed my mind. I told my dad that I did not want to be a lawyer, because they lie too much. My dad talked to me a couple of times about going to college and encouraged me to go to college, but to no avail. It probably would not have mattered if I talked to the school counselor or anyone else about my future, because I had already made up my mind. So, off I went to find my place in this world.

After graduation, I got a job. One of my teachers, Ms. D. recommended me for a job at a fast-food restaurant in Oakland. I went for an interview and got my first job. I worked 10:00 a.m. to 7 p.m. five days a week as a waitress. I liked the job; however, I did not like the city it was in. Oakland was a very busy place with bumper-to-bumper traffic and lots of people every day. I had to take the bus to and from work everyday. It was okay for the summer, because it was still light outside when I would leave work. However, the time would change in the fall and it would be dark by the time I left work to go home. So, after one and a half months working at the restaurant, I quit. I didn't feel safe going to catch the bus in Oakland when it was dark. I did not work for about a month or so after that.

Finally, I did get my own bedroom in my parent's house, but not until everyone either got married or moved out. Some people in my house liked to help themselves to other people's things, so I had a dead bolt put on my bedroom to keep people from coming in my room and taking my things. Back when I was growing up, a lot of young girls would have what was called a "hope chest." In this chest would be things that you would buy or collect for the day you got married, such as dish towels, silverware, dishes, etc. I didn't have a "hope chest" per say, but I did buy and/or collect things for the some day I would get married. I had all kinds of boxes stacked up neatly against the wall all around my room. In these boxes were the "hope chest" things I was collecting. In time, I was not only packing away material things for that "some day," but I began packing my life (my hopes and dreams) away in those boxes and some day never came.

One morning when I was still sleeping, my dad called up the steps to me and told me to get out of bed because a local fast food hoagie shop was hiring people to work for them. My dad wanted me to go and apply for the job. The hoagie shop was a new business and had only been open about six months prior to my applying for the other job. So, I went and applied for the job, and I was hired almost immediately. I started working at the hoagie shop in October 1979 and would spend the next fourteen years of my life there. In the beginning, I really enjoyed my job. I thought that maybe one day I would own my own business. I started out as a short order cook and cashier. Short order cook was my primary job and I felt I was very good at it. Eventually, I had more responsibility such as training new employees, slicing of lunchmeat and vegetables, ordering supplies, tending to repairmen, opening and closing the store or whatever needed to be done. I considered myself a supervisor, but had the responsibility of a manager. The only thing I did not do at my job was the banking aspect.

I liked my boss, the owner of the business, and the people I worked with very much. My pay scale was minimum wage. In time, my boss became more like a mother to me. In search of a mother I found my boss. I trusted my boss more than I would ever trust my own mother. She liked my work, and I thought she was very pleased with what I was doing. I got a few small raises, but I never asked for a raise the whole time I worked for her. Anyway, I felt that I shouldn't have to ask for a raise, she should just give me one, if I was doing such good work. As time went on my boss gave me money aside from my check. It started out at fifty dollars once a month, but by the time I left the business she had just increased the amount of money to two hundred dollars a month. At first, she told me and led me to believe that the money was a gift and not actually included as part of my salary, because she appreciated my work. Once my hourly wage hit three dollars and fifty-five cents in my paycheck, my boss never increased my wage. My wage written on my paycheck stayed at three dollars and fifty-five cents until the day I left that job. I wasn't interested in her money or for that fact in anybody else's either. Due to my own ignorance of finances, I truly had no real sense of what making money really meant and what money's real purpose for life was. One time I even told my boss that I would work for free, if I could. I felt that I was helping her, which was worth more than her money to me. And many times, she would tell me how slow business was and that she was not making very much money, so I also thought she needed the money. Since I was working a lot of overtime, I really didn't need that extra money at the time, so she set up a savings account for me and would put the extra money in the account. I used my parents' car since the time I learned to drive. With the money in my savings account, I was able to pay cash for my first new car.

I admired her and thought she was a very nice person. I thought she had what appeared to be a happy marriage, two happy children, and a good life. This was something that my family did not seem to have. What's more, I thought she really cared about me. We had a very good relationship. But one day just out of the blue, she told me about her secret. She told me that I had to promise not to tell anyone her secret. If I remember correctly, she told me that only her doctor, husband, and a cousin and his wife knew about her secret. Most importantly she did not want her children to know about her secret, because she did not want them to worry about her. My boss's secret was that she had an illness, multiple sclerosis, which can be terminal, but she was doing very well. As a matter of fact, you would have never even known there was something physically wrong with her. She told me that she wanted to live to see her children grow up. I kept her secret in my heart just as she asked and did not tell anyone. Then feeling safe with her, I shared my secret about being raped. I believe she would be only the fourth person that knew at this time. I thought that she believed me at the time. And my family still did not know about my being raped.

Over time, our relationship grew to be more like a mother/daughter relationship. As I got to know her, I know that she did not have the perfect life, but endured a lot of hardships, just like most people. Sometimes, my boss would even tell me that I was just like a daughter to her. Just like my mother, my boss was a perfectionist and she was dying or so she made me believe. My boss also used to say that same phrase my mother did, "when I die." I wanted to protect my boss from dying, just like I wanted to protect my mother. I wanted to take care of her, because I knew she wanted to see her children grow up. If I could have traded and taken her illness, I would have. That's how much I cared about her. I guess I still thought I was invincible, and I truly felt I could have handled her illness very well. At this job, I thought I had found my purpose and reason for living. So, I gave my boss and my job my life. I was at her beck and call. If she said jump, I said how high. Aside from work, I did whatever she asked me to do for her. Some of the things I did would be to get supplies, if we were going to run out before our schedule delivery. I would take her places such as shopping or pick her up if it was snowing. I was never reimbursed for the gas or mileage that came out of my own pocket. Now, I didn't mind doing this because I felt needed, and it was not about money. I enjoyed spending time with her. After all, I did see her as a mother. I worked Monday through Sunday, anywhere from sixty to eighty hours a week or whenever the doors were open. It was not until my last year working for her that I took Monday as a regular day off. Usually, I didn't make plans to do anything, because I thought my boss might need me. If I had plans to go out with my friends or to a family get together and my boss needed me to work, I would cancel my plans and go to work. If someone called to say they couldn't work or did not want to work, I worked. And if I did have plans to do something with my friends or family, I would always tell her where I was going and call and check in to make sure she didn't need me. If she needed me, I came back from wherever I was. I did not have a consistent day off a week, like most people. My day off would usually be if the store was closed or on other rare occasions. Even if I was sick, I usually came to work. For example, when I was twenty-eight years old, I got chicken pox. She didn't believe me at first, so she wanted me to come to her house so she could see and I went. I still went to work the next day, but then she saw that I was really sick and sent me home. I never considered myself to be a sick person and I never called in sick. However, when I was about twenty years old, my right hand basically quit working. It was very painful to do anything with the turning of my wrist, such as sweeping the floor and turning the pancake turner to cook. I had gone to see a doctor and he put a cast on my arm up to the elbow. I had this on for about six weeks, but I still worked. I got the cast off and my wrist was not any better. The doctor at the time thought I had broken my wrist at some point and it never healed. I didn't think the doctor knew what was wrong with the wrist. My boss took it upon herself to call around and find a specialist for me to go to. And I went. The specialist told me that I had something similar to carpal tunnel, and that this disease usually happened in older people between seventy and eighty years old. The doctor said that the bone in my wrist did not grow completely, and that cooking at my job caused a sheath to form over the bone, causing the pain I was having. The doctor gave me several cortisone shots to try and correct the problem. Surgery was also an option, but he felt that the sheath would grow back. Then he said that if the shots didn't work, I would probably have to find another job. One thing the doctor said that I religiously followed was that he told me never to stop using my wrist no matter how painful, because he felt that I would lose the use of my hand altogether. And I listened to his instructions. Eventually, my wrist did get better although every now and it would act up, but I never stopped using my hand. I felt that my boss saved my life by helping me and I was indebted to her.

An essential and important part of the business was being able to cook fast and well. I was able to do both. My boss and her husband did not cook and their children were too young. So, I really felt needed. In my free time, I went to clubs or bars to drink and dance with my friends, but eventually what I had of a social life soon diminished to nothing. Anyway, my appetite for the bar scene was fast fading. My best friend, Sandy, moved to another state and soon got married. To maintain a long distance friendship was hard. One day in a phone conversation with Sandy we got into an argument. I'm not really sure what we were arguing about, but she told me that I was a very difficult person. Well, this hurt me very much, because at the time I was really trying to make some changes in myself. Thinking back to that time, I remember that Sandy came to know Jesus. I remember thinking to myself, oh, she knows God now so I'm not good enough for her. Sandy and I stopped speaking for about three years. I did not take time or have the time to pursue new friendships. My job came first. I ate, drank, and slept my job. Maybe this was part of my need to prove that I was able to make it out in the big world.

As far as a dating relationship goes, I really didn't date much. I didn't believe in dating someone just to say that I was dating. I always dreamed, planned, and talked about getting married. That is all I ever wanted to do, but I wanted the Cinderella fairy tale. You know, Prince Charming coming on his white horse to sweep me away, but in my dream I don't believe I wanted to actually live in the real world, I just wanted the fantasy. Although I had a couple offers of marriage, I never really had a serious relationship or someone I felt I really loved and wanted to spend the rest of my life with. I think one of my issues regarding dating and/or a serious relationship was my self-image. I wanted to have the perfect body and weight. Being naïve and very impressionable, I usually believed what people told me, especially my boss. One time, I really liked a customer who frequented our store. He was actually a brother of two of the employees. I remember how much I wanted and believed he could like me and that I was good enough for him to ask me out, but that never happened. Anyway, my boss knew I liked this person. If I remember correctly, I recall her telling me that men wanted someone they can hang on their arm, meaning men wanted someone skinny, pretty, and someone they could show off. My boss told me that I could never be married. She didn't explain what she meant by her statement, but I took it to mean that I was not good enough to be somebody's wife. I think I believed that I had to have the perfect body and weight to be loved by a man. And from my boss's statement I believe she was insinuating the same thing. The dating scene in my life became non-existent.

As time went on, my boss became verbally abusive to me. Her anger was just like my mother's, but maybe at times even worse. My boss would become so enraged at times.

For example, one Friday night we were extremely busy at work. We started running out of supplies - lunchmeat, bread, vegetables, etc. Then, my boss went into one of her rages and began screaming and yelling at me. I cannot recall exactly what happened, but I thought I was doing my best. It had been a long day and I had already been working more than ten hours. We were out in front behind the counter, but the customers and employees had a clear view of what was happening. My boss kept screaming at me, and I went in the back and started crying. I cried at work a good bit. It seemed like whatever went wrong, I was to blame. I could not do anything perfect or good enough. My boss did come back and apologize and I think she even cried with me, but this was only one of the many different times she went into a rage with me. I know that some of the employees felt badly for me, and they would tell me that I was the business, meaning that if my boss did not have me, there would be no business and she couldn't find someone like me ever. But the employees did not understand, because I knew her secret. I made excuses as to why she treated me like she did saying things like, "It's o.k.; you just don't understand." I painted a picture of how wonderful she was and at times she could be. She would shower me with some gifts for holidays and my birthday. Also, I had lived in anger and rage just like this all my life, so what was the difference. This was normal for me, because I could handle anger like this. As a matter of fact, my boss was probably worse than my mother.

My boss was also emotionally abusive. My boss used to tell me how stupid I was. One day, when she told me that I was so stupid, I started to cry. I did not know why she said this to me. I thought to myself if I am so stupid, why do you call me to come and take care of things when something breaks or something goes wrong. She tried to console me, and I asked my boss, "Why do you always call me stupid?"

And she said something like, "Oh, that's just a saying and I don't mean it." My boss would withhold her love and approval from me. She would tell me she loved me like a daughter. If I was good and everything was going well, then she would love me. But if I did something wrong or that she did not approve of, then she would withdraw her love and approval. She knew how much I wanted and needed her to love me and approve of me. I was afraid of losing her love. Now, I was by no means a perfect employee, and I had many faults. I was very moody and used the "silent treatment" to try and prove my point, but it didn't work. Although I had my faults, I felt that I was a trustworthy, loyal, and dedicated employee. One thing I did do was give this job and my boss my heart and one-hundred percent plus. I always wanted to be perfect and do everything perfectly for her.

Many times I would ask my boss to tell me how I could do things better and she would say, "You do every-thing right," and then it would go right back to the same old thing. Still the things I did were not right. The yelling and screaming continued. Her words and her actions with me were so contradictory.

My boss was a very manipulative person. The things that she did for you or someone else usually benefited her more than the other person. For example, she might give you a free lunch, but in return she knew that there was so much more you could do for her. I felt she was insincere a lot and pretended to be someone she was not. One time she made friends with a very nice lady. This lady had some hard times, but was very religious. I don't know if this lady was a Christian or not, but she appeared to be. My boss had lunch with her occasionally. One day, my boss was having lunch with this lady and she expressed a desire to take a class that was coming up soon, but she didn't have the money. I believe this lady wanted to take a Bible class. In talking with my boss, she wanted to pay for the lady to go to this class, but she didn't want the lady to know that she had that kind of money to give her. So my boss told the lady that she won the lottery and was giving her the money she won to pay for the class. This was a nice gesture, but my perception and knowledge of my boss's relationship with this lady that she was her religious good luck charm, because this lady was very religious and spiritual. My boss also wanted people to think that she was so thoughtful and nice and at times she may have been. My boss always used to tell me what a "good actress" she was when she would play her games, and as I think back, she <u>was</u>. She knew how to play the game and win.

When all the hurt would build up inside for me, and I could not take her abuse, I would tell my boss, "I quit." I could not tell you the many hundreds of times I told her I quit, but never followed through. By quitting my job, I guess I thought it would hurt her like she hurt me, but I was wrong. I was definitely immature. You may think to yourself, why did I not quit? Well, it was probably because I thought she would not be able to keep her business going and that she would die. I did truly believe that she needed me, and I wanted her to live to see her children grow up.

My boss liked to play mind games too. For example, one time she told me that she did not want to name me manager, because she was at the store all the time and she didn't really need a manager. I accepted that. Then when a guy named George who was working for her quit for the first time, she had a little celebration naming me her manager. But she never really considered me a manager, in my opinion, simply because I was not good enough. I believe she only did this to pacify me so that I would not leave too. Even if she referred to me as her manager, which was not often, it would benefit her somehow; it used to make me sick, because I knew she was not sincere.

My boss and I ate out frequently together, and I never had to pay my part of the bill. One time we were eating at

Wendy's, if I remember correctly. My boss was paying attention to the work (i.e. how they were attending to customers' needs, having a pleasant personality, and making sure that the food on the salad bar was neat and fresh) of one of the people that was in a management position there. She commented to me that she wished that her manger (meaning me) would be like that. She wanted me to believe that she really saw me as someone she considered good enough to be her manager, but I was not.

My boss was very controlling, just like my mother. My ignorance as to what was normal and what was not was something else! My boss also thought I was very pretty, but not skinny enough. The only time I was what I would consider thin, was the first year I worked for her. She approved of me very much, but as time went on and I gained weight, I even felt she was ashamed of me. An example of her control over me and my need for her approval was that one time she made an indirect comment on my wearing jeans. I went to her house to pick her up, because I was taking her somewhere and I had jeans on. I can still remember the way she looked at me in my jeans. Her facial expression and look spoke volumes to me. She said that "only skinny girls wore jeans" and stated how she didn't wear jeans either. I would never forget the feeling of shame, embarrassment, and disgust I felt, because of what she said and how she looked at me. After that day, I never wore jeans again. It was not until the past four years that I started to wear jeans again. I so wanted to conform to what she wanted me to be, and I was so blinded by my need for her approval and love. I believed she also used her love as a means of control. My boss would often tell me that she loved me. One day I did something wrong (I don't recall what I did.) and she was very angry with me. I followed her around the store just like a puppy dog, because I wanted to know what I did wrong. For some reason, I think I asked her if she still loved me and she said no, but just for the moment. I was devastated, because I needed her to love me.

In the early years of the business, my boss would tell how no one deserved to have the business more than I did and made me believe that one day the business would be mine, but she did not mean this either. The guy George came back to work for my boss. Just let me mention here that I liked and respected George as a person and co-worker very much, and we had a good working relationship. Anyway, when George returned to work for my boss, she gave him a contract. I did not have one. She gave him the first option to buy the store, if she was going to sell it. She gave him two weeks' paid vacation and paid holidays. I had worked for her longer than George and I only got one week paid vacation, no paid holidays and no benefits at all. She betrayed me by giving George first option to buy the store. And yes, I was hurt. But in time I realized that my job was going nowhere, and I did not feel that owning this business was what I really wanted to do. I felt that I had so much more to give than I was giving. The only problem was that I didn't know what I wanted to do, but something had to change.

On Monday, October 8, 1990, about 1:20 a.m. my father died of lung cancer. This was the turning point in my life. I called my boss to let her know that my dad had died. I told her that my dad would be laid out at the funeral home on Monday night. Due to one of my brother's and his family's living out of state, we waited until Tuesday, to have my dad laid out at the funeral home. I got back to work that Friday and I remember telling my boss why we waited until Tuesday to lay my dad out, and she said, "So you didn't have to have Monday off." I just remember thinking how mean and insensitive she was toward me. I remember telling her at some point that I saw her show more compassion to a total stranger. Things were not going to get any better.

Just about one month prior to my dad's death, my cousin and I signed up to take a beginner's college computer class on Wednesday nights. Now, I thought this was a good night to have class, because I did not work Wednesday nights. The people that were employed were very dependable. After a couple of weeks of class, my boss started scheduling me to work on Wednesday nights for no reason. Eventually, I quit taking the class, which I believe was her intention, so I could be completely available to work for her.

In December of 1990, my sister Gracie and I were at my mother's house cleaning for the holidays. This would be our first Christmas without Dad. While we were cleaning, Gracie asked me if I had seen what Dad left in the Bible for us and I said no. She told me that my brother Drew found it the day of dad's funeral. Gracie got the Bible and opened it up to the Book of John, which was also my dad's name. I thought this was so awesome. She showed me all the things Dad had underlined in the book for us to know. As I read all that was underlined in the Book of John, I started crying. It was then that I knew God had a plan for my life. The Book of John in the Bible is about salvation. A couple years later, my brother Drew, who was a Christian at the time, told me about finding what my dad left in the Bible. He said that on the day of my dad's funeral he was looking through the Bible and found a bunch of verses underlined in the Book of John. Drew told me he asked my mother if she had been studying the Bible, and she said no and told him that my dad had been fooling around with it. Now my dad was not a Christian that we know of, but my brother said he believed that my dad did receive Jesus in his heart from reading the things he found in the Book of John. I told my brother how much that Bible meant to me and today I have the Bible my dad left.

In October 1991, just a year after my father's death, I moved out of my parents' house for the first time in my life. I had just turned thirty years old. The woman I worked for

80

helped me to find an apartment about a half a mile away from my job. Although my boss probably helped me more for her own benefit, God had a better plan. With some of the money I saved, my boss helped me to decorate the apartment. For a first time apartment, it was really beautiful. I told my mother I was going to move out, and at the time she thought this would be good for me. But when I actually moved out, she was not happy. The day I moved, my mom was in the house, but when I went to say good-bye to her she was gone. I searched the house and I could not find her. Once again, she disappeared. I moved into the apartment toward the end of October. Within the first couple days of my being in my new apartment, my boss stopped by to visit me. She hugged me and said to me that someone must be praying for me. I guess, because my apartment was really nice for a first apartment. I can still feel the glare of her eyes when she said "someone must be praying for me." Her statement made me feel as if I did not deserve anything nice. I just knew there had to be a better life than what I was living. It was in that apartment that I began searching for it.

My search began by my wanting to not be so negative. So, I started by reading self-help and motivational books. Now, I was not much of a reader, in fact, I hated reading. I remember in elementary and middle school that I read two books. One was *The Key to the Treasure* and the other was *The Borrowers*. Every time I had to do a book report, I wrote a report on one of these two books. I guess the nuns never figured out what I did, because they never said anything to me. Anyway, at the time I really saw how negative I was. I wanted to have a more positive outlook and attitude. If I remember correctly, the first book I read was toward gaining a better knowledge of a better life, *The Power of Positive Thinking* by Norman Peale. I loved that book and continued to read other self-help books. Although I went to church, I started watching religious services on television such as Robert Schuler and Charles Stanley. Also, I listened to Christian radio talk shows featuring Chuck Swindoll.

God started to really work on me. About the year 1992, I decided that cussing like a sailor was not becoming of who I was. I began praying that God would help me to stop cussing. My plan was to start replacing cuss words with ordinary words such as sugar plum or darn. The plan was working, but it was going to take some time to change this habit. My boss told me about a little, pocket-sized pamphlet her friend told her about called *Daily Word* published by a religious group called Unity. This pamphlet had inspirational stories and scripture. You can get this pamphlet on a monthly basis through the mail. I called and ordered the pamphlet to come to my house. I enjoyed this pamphlet and looked forward to reading the stories in it. In the spring of 1993, I decided to go on a spiritual retreat. Unity sponsored a week long retreat that was held at Unity Village in Lee's Summit, Missouri. So, I made reservations to go. The retreat was great. One of the things that stood out to me about Unity Village was the profound peace you felt in this village. The peace was truly indescribable and beyond words, and I was not the only one that felt this way. Some ladies and I had the opportunity to do some sightseeing. We hired a limousine to take us touring. When the driver came to get us, he commented about the unbelievable peace you feel when you drive into the village. The peace was definitely something you took notice of. At Unity, people were praying around the clock for people's needs and prayer requests that came not only from people there in the village, but people mailed or called in prayer requests from everywhere. Never having experienced this type of atmosphere, I was very impressed with Unity. They taught about God and His healing power and were based on the teachings of Charles and Myrtle Fillmore. Unity had a school where you can go and be trained in the beliefs of the Unity religion and become a teacher. I was really considering going to Unity and becoming a teacher. I thought it would be something I would enjoy. The retreat ended and I returned to Pittsburgh and to my job.

As I continued in the day to day activities of work, I was so discontented and unhappy. I recall an incident happening where someone told me something and I believed them. Later, I found out that it was not true. Due to being naïve and lacking in knowledge, I would usually believe anything anyone said, unless I knew they had lied to me before. I was angry at myself for believing what was said without questioning it. I felt stupid and felt like people were walking all over me. So, I decided I was not going to feel this way anymore. I remember praying to God and asking Him to teach me to discern the difference between truth and evil. This would be my new weapon against lies and evil.

Some of the things that God showed me were the lies and deceptions of my boss. I began questioning her about the salary of my co-worker, George. My confrontation about this matter was something to the effect of how was George making ends meet with a salary similar to mine with a wife and children to support. I now had my own apartment and was finding it hard to make it at times. When I lived with my parents, I paid them some money for rent, but not much. I knew that George got two weeks' paid vacation and paid holidays. He worked nine to five, Monday through Friday and an occasional Saturday, so I didn't have to. Then, I found out he was being paid salary, whereas I had an hourly wage. I questioned my boss and kept questioning her, because I wanted to know exactly how much he was being paid. God was opening my eyes to the truth. I knew George was making more money than I, and he worked less time than I did. A lot of the money I was making was in overtime. My boss beat around the bush when I questioned her. Finally, she told me that George did make a little more than me, but not much. And with the money she paid me that was supposed to be a gift, she said that our salaries were about the same. Today, I know that was a lie. For me, this confrontation was not about money, but about the truth. See, I thought that as long as I was able to work and get overtime then I would do whatever it took. Shortly after our conversation, my boss started cutting my hours. All she had to do was tell me the truth, and I would have been perfectly happy, but she couldn't do that.

I started catching my boss in more lies. One day, she told me that she was being audited by the IRS. Then she went on to tell me that someone from the unemployment office, either called her on the phone or told her in person that a girl came to their office. She was indicating that this girl was there at the unemployment office to get her into trouble. My boss described the girl as being me. I told her that I would never do anything like that. Anyway, I didn't even know where the unemployment office was. Then, about a week or so went by, forgetting what she told me previously, my boss came to me and said that she talked to the owner of the franchise that she owned. He told her that the IRS does random auditing and that it was nothing to worry about. So, I said to her something to the effect that there was never a girl that showed up at the unemployment office and she went off into some ridiculous story. Then, I simply said to her, "So you lied to me." I said no more and turned and walked away. My secret weapon was surely working. God was opening my eyes to all the lies. Now at this time in my life, I know that she had something to be concerned about, because if I had done what she said I did, I could have probably gotten her into trouble. My boss told me that I had changed. I believed she meant that I had changed for the worse. At the time, I didn't feel like I had changed at all, and not for the worst. Now, as I look back, I did change, but it was for the good. I'm sure my boss didn't like the fact that I did not trust her like I used to.

In December 1993, my brother, Drew and his family came to Pittsburgh for the Christmas holidays. We were having breakfast at my sister Charity's house. Drew, whom I mentioned earlier was the only Christian in our family, began witnessing to me, and talking about Jesus. I proceeded to tell Drew about some of the things I had become aware of about people in our church who called themselves Christians. At some point in our conversation, Drew stopped me and said; "Betsy, do you know the Lord?" Not really sure what it meant to truly know Jesus in your heart, I told him I didn't know. Drew said that I couldn't know all that I was telling him and not know the Lord. After Drew explained to me about Jesus, I told him I guess I did know the Lord and he congratulated me. I believe it was through the television ministry of Charles Stanley that I came to know the Lord. Charles Stanley usually gives an invitation to receive Jesus as your Lord and Savior. At the end of his program, I know I said the invitation more than once, but I guess I did not understand what it meant or felt like to receive Jesus in your heart. I was not in a Christian environment and did not have anyone to talk to about this experience. All I knew for sure at the time is that I was changing for the better, and God was answering my prayers.

My brother Drew talked to me about finding a Christian church. He recommended an Alliance Church, which was the denomination he and his family belonged to. Now I was still interested in the Unity religion and was thinking about going on another retreat to Unity Village in the spring. I was discussing the Unity religion with Drew and he showed me a pamphlet with facts about the errors of this religion. After seeing the facts, the Unity religion was not the right direction to go. I trusted my brother's direction and no longer pursued the Unity religion.

In January of 1994, I really wanted to find a better job. I thought about opening my own business. I was heading in the direction of opening a daycare center or an at home gift basket business, however, neither seemed to be the right thing to do. I was still searching for my place in the world. God started turning my mind toward the things that are of Him. For instance, I began frequenting Christian book stores, just wanting to be around things that were based on God. I remember one of the first verses God gave me. I was in a Christian book store and there was a picture of a grand-fatherly looking man and a boy sailing on troubled waters. There was a verse inscribed on the picture, Jeremiah 29:11, which says; "For I know the plans I have for you, declares the Lord, plans to prosper you and not to harm you, plans to give you hope and a future." This verse truly touched me and I placed it in my heart. The part that really touched me was "I will not harm you." Those words comforted my soul. I had been hurt so much and I very much needed that comfort and the assurance of those words. I consider this verse my theme verse.

Things at my job were still on a downhill slide. In May of 1994, things really began to change spiritually for me. One evening, I came home from work. I remember it had been a perfectly beautiful spring day. I sat down in my favorite chair in my living room. I just sat there perfectly still. Everything was peaceful and quiet with no interference of the worldly noises such as television or radio. I was just resting and I began looking around my living room at the pictures hanging on my wall. Then, in the quiet of the evening, a voice (not audible) came to me and said, "Can you give all this up and come follow me?"

As I was looking around, without hesitation, I said, "Yes." At that moment, the perfect peace and calmness I felt was nothing I could ever describe. When I heard the voice speak somehow I knew in my heart it was the voice of the Lord talking to me and this was new for me. So, I did not tell anyone about this experience, because I thought people would think I was crazy. I felt like no one would ever under-stand what hearing God's voice was like for me.

Then, I decided that I needed to be in a Christian environment, because I needed more of God. My plan was to go and live with my brother Drew and his family in North Carolina. My boss was not happy with my decision. She tried to talk me out of moving to North Carolina and she succeeded. My boss proposed that I go to North Carolina and visit to see if I would like it there. Next, she said that when I came back from my visit with my brother, and if I still was not happy, then she would let me go, and not say anything to me. So, I thought this was great, because then I would not feel guilty about leaving her. That night when I went home to my apartment I knew my decision to not go and live with my brother, and instead just visit, was wrong. I had gone to bed, closed my eyes, and was just about to fall fast asleep. Then, this face appeared to me laughing hysterically at me. It was the face of the devil. I awoke terrified. I looked around my room to see if anyone was there. I had never experienced anything like this before and never did again. It was then that I knew for sure that I had made the wrong decision to stay in Pittsburgh. I paid a high price for my decision. My boss began what I would call withdrawing her love and approval from me. She would always tell me pretty much everything that was going on in both the business and her life, but now she started excluding me. Previously, when she would go away for the weekend, I would be the one she would tell, well not anymore.

In June of 1994, I visited my brother in North Carolina. While I was visiting my brother, he received a pamphlet in the mail from Toccoa Falls College saying that Christian Counseling was now a major at the college. Toccoa Falls College is a Christian college in Georgia. I had seen the pamphlet and told my brother that is what I wanted to do. He told me I could have the pamphlet. I enjoyed my visit with my brother and his family, but I was not sure I would really like living in North Carolina. I returned to Pittsburgh to my job. I unpacked my suitcase and left the pamphlet for Toccoa Falls College in the suitcase. I placed the suitcase by my television.

I was still unhappy and discontent with my life in general, still thinking there had to be more to life than this. It felt like I just existed. I felt trapped because I had so much more to give than I was giving. Then, I decided I would go to a local community college for psychology. Psychology was always something that fascinated me, because I always wanted to know why people did what they did. I went and signed up at the community college for one class. A couple of weeks later, around the middle of July, I received a statement in the mail for payment of the class. I remember sitting in my favorite chair reading the statement. As I read the statement there was strange pressure on my heart. It felt as if someone put their hand gently on my heart and pushed softly on it. I knew that to go to the community college was not the right thing to do. At that moment, I remembered the Toccoa Falls College pamphlet in my suitcase by the television. I got out of my chair, went and got the suitcase, and took the pamphlet out of it. I called Toccoa Falls College and requested information about the college and the programs they offered. About a week later, I had not received any information yet, so I called Toccoa Falls College again, because I thought it was taking too long for the information. This time, I had a conversation with an admissions' counselor. Her name was Julie. I inquired about the requirements for admission to the college and the counseling program. Julie and I discussed the fact that I was thirty-two years old and had been out of school for fifteen years. I told Julie that I had never taken a SAT (required test for admission for college). I told Julie that I would never be able to pass that test. The good news was that I would not have to take the test, due to my age. As part of the entrance requirement to get into Toccoa Falls College, you had to write a Christian testimony. Julie and I discussed my being a new Christian and not being baptized. Being baptized was very important to me. Julie told me that I could get baptized at the college. I was so excited about this wonderful new opportunity. Now, if you remember, I never wanted to go to college, but God was busy at work. Julie sent me an application for college.

As soon as I received the application, I filled it out, did my best at writing a Christian testimony (remember English was not my best subject), and sent the information immediately. The fall semester was to begin August 25, 1994, and I had to hurry if I wanted to get in. Along with the application came a pamphlet by Charles Stanley. If I remember correctly, the pamphlet was called *Knowing God's Will*. This pamphlet by Charles Stanley was confirmation to me that Toccoa Falls College was where God wanted me to be. A week or so went by and I did not hear from Julie. I called to check on the status of my application to see if I would be accepted for the fall semester. I believe I talked to one of the other admissions' counselors, because Julie was not in the office. She told me that the committee that approved the applications for school was out on summer break, but was due to meet in about a week. You see, I was being very persistent, which I am by nature, because I wanted to give my boss at least a four-week notice of my resignation, because I felt this was fair. A week came and went and still no word from Julie. Again, I called the college to check on my application status, still no word. It was now about four weeks before the fall semester would begin. I had to make a decision as to whether I should quit my job, move to Georgia, and go to Toccoa Falls College. Time was getting short and I had to make a decision without knowing if I would be accepted into college for the fall or not. Now, I would only be able to give my boss about a three-week notice of my resignation. After work one day, I came home, and still there was no news from Toccoa Falls College. So, I started thinking about the decision I had to make. I remember going to my phone and before picking up the phone I said something to myself like this: "God, I work for you now, and you won't be mean to me or yell and scream at me." On that note, I reached down to pick up the phone, and called Julie at Toccoa Falls College, and told her I was coming to Georgia. My intention was to go to Toccoa Falls College for four years, get my Bachelor's Degree in Psychology, and return to Pittsburgh.

Now, there were some major circumstances that I was facing with my decision to go to Toccoa Falls College. First, I knew no one in Georgia, with the exception of the admissions' counselor I had been talking with for a few weeks. Second, at the time of my decision, I still did not know if I would be accepted into school for the fall semester or where the money to pay for school would come from. Third, I did not have a place to live. Next, I did not have a job to go to. Last, I was having major car trouble. I had a 1990 Eagle Summit that needed the engine replaced. I had to go to the dealer and fight for a new engine, because I had engine trouble within the first two years of having the car. I felt I was justified in having them replace the engine for free, because I had kept up with the maintenance on the car. So, with less than four weeks to go to Georgia, the dealership I bought my car from agreed to replace the engine in my car for free. I explained to them that I was moving to Georgia and I had to have my car back in a few weeks. God was really making way for me to move to Georgia.

So, I gave my boss a three-week notice of resignation with Sunday, August 21, 1994 being my last day of work. Again, she was not happy with my decision to move to Georgia and go to school. So, she tried once again to talk me out of moving. One night, I was driving my boss home and discussing my leaving. I told her that I could not help her anymore and I didn't know what else to do for her. At my job one day during this three-week notice, my boss asked to speak to me. So, we went out in the dining room area and sat in one of the booths. She started talking to me about leaving and asked me why I was leaving. I simply told her that I wanted a better life. Well, I'm sure she didn't believe me. Anyway, if I remember correctly she started talking about my being concerned about what George was being paid. I told you about him earlier. Now, I did not, and was not asking my boss for a raise. I just wanted the truth, and for her to be fair to me. Our conversation went on, and she said to me that I was not worth anymore than she paid me. Well, that was the knife that cut right through my heart. On that note, I got up from the table and said, "That's it; it is over." I walked back to do my job.

My boss stopped me and said; "Don't worry; God will take care of me."

I looked at her with all sincerity and said, "He will." And now my decision to leave was final. God gave me perfect peace. I think I could say in all fairness that my boss usually underestimated me, and that was okay, but this time she underestimated the power of God.

With only a little more than three weeks to tie up loose ends, pack, and empty my apartment, my schedule was pretty tight. At work, I still gave my best plus, until the end. The word from God was that I was only to take my clothes, my car, and some basic necessities to Georgia. I tried to sell some of my furniture in my apartment so that I could have some more money. Then, I had to pack everything else and find a storage place. About a week before I was to leave Pittsburgh, I received the great news from Julie that I was accepted at Toccoa Falls College for the fall semester. Things were falling into place, and I was excited.

My job ended and soon it was time to leave Pittsburgh. My car was still in the shop being repaired and would not be ready in time for me to leave. But God had a great plan. The dealership offered to give me a loaner car absolutely free of charge for as long as it took for them to fix my car. My car would not have been big enough to take all my things. God worked all the details out perfectly.

My family had a going away party for me. I was going to miss everyone, especially my nieces and nephew, because they were like my children. My nephew Paul still lived with my mom, and I talked to him about my leaving. I asked Paul if he knew why I was leaving, and he told me that it was because I wanted to be happy. I told him that I wanted a better life. I guess I was feeling guilty, but he understood. My friend George, from work, called and said that he had a card for me. Usually, when someone left our work that had been with us for a while, our boss and employees pitched in with money for a gift. When I went to pick up the card, George told me that the gift was from him and the other employees. He said that my boss did not participate. I was hurt, because I believed she would help me go to school. She could not be happy for me. I guess that was my punishment for leaving her. At thirty-two years of age, with about eight hundred dollars to my name, no place to live, no job, and no acquaintances in Georgia, on Wednesday, August 24, 1994, I left Pittsburgh and began my journey.

Chapter 6

A Whole New World

"For I know the plans I have for you, declares the Lord,
plans to prosper you and not to harm you, plans to give
you hope and a future." Jeremiah 29:11

With a stopover in Virginia to see my friend Sandy and her family, I arrived in Georgia on Thursday, August 25, 1994 around 4:30 p.m. As I was driving toward Toccoa, which was the city where Toccoa Falls College was located, I came to a part in the road that was somewhat of an incline before you head downhill. As I approached the point of the incline, the sun appeared to be setting right on the hill. It was the most breathtaking sight, a perfect moment in time capturing the beauty of the day. When I passed through the high point of the incline, I felt like I passed through to a whole new world and a rush of fresh air had just been transmitted through my body. I felt just like Aladdin and Princess Jasmine from the Disney Movie *Aladdin*, when they soared through the sky on an enchanted carpet ride. I had such a tremendous feeling of peace and joy that was beyond words.

That moment made my heart skip a beat in time. It was as if God were telling me, "Welcome to the place where I want you to be." An opportunity for a place to live opened up. So, I headed into town to meet with a couple that I could possibly rent a room from. I had intended to stay in a hotel until I found a place to live, but this couple let me stay at their house. They offered to let me rent a room in their house, and this would be my home for now. Since I was late in getting to Toccoa Falls College, I signed up for school on Friday, August 26, 1994. It was a challenging day signing up for classes, taking placement tests, and touring the campus. I got some serious exercise that day walking all over the campus. I officially started school that Monday. I didn't do well on the placement tests, so I had to take the basic reading and English classes. I signed up to take classes full-time. I was so impressed with the faculty, and staff at Toccoa Falls College. I was truly blessed with some wonderful teachers. And now I would be in a Christian environment.

I began searching for a job, which I needed immediately. My money that I had would not last long. At the time, I didn't realize I probably could have applied for unemployment until I got a job. But as I think back to that time, applying for unemployment was not God's plan. I would have had to have contact with my ex-boss and I know that was not what God had in mind. I applied at Wal-Mart, because I thought this would be good for me. There was an opening in the snack shop which was great, since I had experience in restaurant work. It took quite a few weeks to get the job. I didn't begin work until the end of September and did not receive a paycheck until October. Financially, this would be challenging. I would work at Wal-Mart full-time. My first day working in the snack shop was very stressful and appeared to be traumatic for me. I was shocked by my emotional response to the job. I didn't like working with food at all now. A cashier wanted to switch job positions with me, and so we switched. God now had everything falling into place: adjustment to school, a place to stay, and a job. Going back to school after fifteen years of being out of school was a serious challenge for me, but a good one. I wanted to prove to some people that I was not stupid, probably my ex-boss in particular. I set for myself a goal that would be unreachable, but I didn't think so. I wanted to graduate from college with a 4.0 grade point average (GPA).

Now, having a limited vocabulary that was very much Pittsburgese, I was grammatically challenged. For instance, take the word syllabus. I had no clue what that meant, and I could not even guess. A dictionary was definitely on my list of books to buy. As a matter of fact, I believe it was required for my reading class. My professor for reading was awesome. She was so kind, helpful, and never made me feel stupid, even though I had a lot to learn. I inquired as to how I could go about increasing my vocabulary. And she was more than helpful in making recommendations as to how I could go about doing this. Also, God was working in my heart removing the things from my vocabulary that were not of Him. That was the cuss words. I told you earlier that I prayed for God to help me to stop using cuss words. After I got here to Georgia, cussing was no longer a problem for me. I stopped completely, and better yet, God did not even allow the cuss words to enter into my thoughts. And I did not like to hear anyone cuss while talking to me. If someone did cuss while speaking to me, I would just try to shut out that part of the conversation. God did answer my prayer.

Coming to Georgia was a completely new experience for me although I loved to travel, and have visited many different states. I considered coming to Georgia the biggest risk of my life and so out of character for me. I left my safe and secluded home life in Pittsburgh to come to a place where I did not know anyone. I did not realize that Georgia had a language all its own, and I had a language barrier to work through.

Some of the folks here spoke a language that I found hard to decipher or what I would consider hillbilly talk. Being one who spoke Pittsburgese, I have no room to complain, but I want to say it sure was different. For example, one day a little girl and her dad came through my line at Wal-Mart. The little girl told me how their doorknob had "tore up." It took me a minute, but I understood what the little girl meant by the way she said it. Now, I would say the doorknob broke. I could not help but smile at the little girl, because she was so adorable with the way she talked.

Communicating my needs with Pittsburgese was at times challenging. For instance, one time I had gone to the college book store in search of gumbands. So, I asked the store clerk if she had any gumbands. She looked at me totally dumbfounded. I looked at her the same way. Again, I repeated to the clerk what I was looking for, and she still didn't get it. At a loss for words to use to explain what I wanted, I told the clerk that I needed the thing that you use to put in your hair to make a pony tail. Then, she said, "Oh you mean a rubber band." Well, I certainly would not have known to say rubber band, because in Pittsburgh the word is gumband. Another example was when I went to a restaurant, I had asked for some ice tea. The waitress or waiter would look at me like I was crazy. It took me some time to figure out that I had to say sweet tea, which was the same as ice tea. Oh yeah, and everybody waves to you here in Georgia. This I did not know. I would be driving along, and people would just wave to me. I would look at them like who are you, because I don't know you. I soon figured out it was just that good old Southern hospitality. As I mentioned earlier, when I lived up North, people used to ask me if I came from the South. Funny, now I was living in the South and had to learn to speak Southern. Quite a few people I met did not believe I really came from the North, because they felt I talked just like a Southerner, and fit in well. It was a little adjustment, but eventually I got it.

Located on Toccoa Falls College Campus is a one-hundred-eighty-six foot tall water falls. I loved going to the falls, as we called it, listening to the sound of the water falling, being still, and wanting to hear from God. Remember, being a new Christian, I had not been baptized yet. Being baptized was something I felt I really needed to do. So, I inquired about getting baptized. It just so happened that in September there was going to be a baptism held at the falls. I took the necessary steps toward baptism and on September 18, 1994, I was baptized at the falls along with eleven other people who were following God's command to be baptized. It was a most wonderful experience. At Toccoa Falls College, I felt I was able to be myself. I didn't have to have my guard up all the time. I met some wonderful people, and had awesome teachers who were highly qualified.

One day on one of my frequent trips to the falls, across the waterfalls appeared a beautiful rainbow. The rainbow became my sign from God that He didn't forget about me. And it was here at the falls that God was telling me that it was time to deal with my abuse issues. I did not think my abuse ever or would ever interfere with my living a normal life, but I knew I had to deal with my past in order for me to do what God wanted me to do. But, who could help me? I prayed to God and asked Him to show me what to do. God answered. He led me to go talk to one of my professors, Dr. M. I went to her office to see if I could talk to her and she was not in. I left her a message saying that I needed to talk with her. Being the persistent person I am, I went back to her office a little later. Dr. M. was in and able to see me. I let her know that I was there to see her, because I needed help in dealing with my abuse issues. I remember crying, and telling her that what scared me most was that I could have hurt someone else, because of what happened to me.

This was a devastating thought. I was terrified. Dr. M. was going to possibly try to arrange an appointment with a counselor from her church or give thought to how she could help me. Emotionally, I felt I was doing very well. For the first time in my life, I thought my emotions were more balanced than ever, and not extreme one way or the other, but I did not have something strange happen to me. One day, in one of my classes the teacher had just taken roll. He had told our class about one of his family members who was seriously ill. He said he had to do a lot of things and appeared to be in much distress. I had to make-up a test for his class. So, thinking I was being helpful, I went up to the teacher and told him that I would take the test whenever it was convenient for him. Then, he literally screamed at me. Being caught off guard, I never expected that response from him or anyone else. I almost went into traumatic distress. I was in shock, and frozen in fear. At the time, I was not really aware of what was happening to me. But I think I can trace my response to this situation back to my traumatic experience in kindergarten, when the teacher screamed at me. Finally, I regained my composure and returned to my seat. Later, the teacher apologized to me for his actions.

Now, I was still driving the loaner car from the dealership in Pennsylvania. Finally, early in October my car was ready for me to pick up. My sister-in-law, Mar and her mother were going to come to Georgia and bring me my car so I did not have to make a trip to Pittsburgh and miss school. When they got here, we received word that a long time family friend, and one of my sister Charity's best friends, had passed away. So, I decided to go to Pittsburgh just for the day to attend the funeral and then return to Georgia. While in Pittsburgh, I stopped at my old place of work to say hi to everyone. My ex-boss used a couple choice words and told me to get out and never come back. I was hurt at what she said, but this may have been for the best.

In the meantime, my living arrangements were not working out. I met a lady named Jody. Jody and I got along very well. We became good friends. Jody was aware of my living situation. She told me about her apartment that she shared with another girl. Jody told me that she would talk to her landlord to see if I could move in with them. In November 1994, I moved into their apartment. I thought this was good, because we were close in age. Also, Jody and I worked together. There were only two bedrooms in the apartment, so Jody and I shared a room. I was just working at Wal-Mart enough to make ends meet. Dr. M. was still trying to arrange counseling services for me, but there would be a twenty-five dollar fee for counseling services. I was not able to pay for services. Dr. M. said that Toccoa Falls hired a full-time counselor to help deal with the needs of the students. If my memory serves me right, Dr. M. said that the counselor was not starting counseling sessions until January. Counseling services would be free of charge to all Toccoa Falls students. Dr. M. suggested that I write to her, and she would help me as much as she could. I did not like writing down my thoughts and feelings, but I did write to Dr. M. and on occasion, Dr. M. would see me to discuss my situation in her office. For the time being, this was how I was receiving help.

Sometime in November, I got word from the financial department that there was a problem with my financial aid. So, I went to see what the problem was. My financial aid adviser told me that I had not sent in some required paper-work to Pennsylvania. Tending to the situation, I filled out the necessary paperwork and sent it to Pennsylvania to be processed. Prior to finals that fall semester, I got word that I would not be able to take my finals, and I would not be able to return to school for the spring semester, because my school bill was not paid yet. Well, needless to say this was not going to happen. My friend Jody suggested that I speak to the vice-president of the college, and so I did. One day after chapel, which was a required part of school, I talked to the vice-president. I explained my situation to him. Then, boldly I said to him something to the effect that he was not going to tell me that I could not come back next semester, and I was going to take my finals. The vice-president then prayed with me. I checked with the financial aid office. They told me that I would be receiving the financial aid; it was just going to get there late. I remember telling the financial aid adviser that God was going to pay my school bill in full. I said that God brought me here, and He knew I did not have the money to pay for school. Today, I still believe that God will pay my school debt in full one day soon.

My sister Charity and some of my family members pitched in to buy me a plane ticket to go to Pittsburgh for the Christmas holidays that year. So, taking things upon myself without direction from God, I made reservations, and got my ticket to visit my family for the Christmas holidays. I was very reliant on myself, and not God. Well, I went to my job, and asked my boss if I could have time off for the Christmas holidays. My boss flat out told me no! I explained to him that I had already bought a plane ticket to go to Pittsburgh. My boss told me that no one was allowed to take off for the Christmas holidays, not even him. He told me that if I did take off at Christmas then I would not have a job to come back to. When God closed that door, I really heard it slam. I should have sought God's direction before I bought the ticket, but I did not. This would be one of many lessons that God would teach me about self-reliance. I could not afford to lose my job. So, I had to call my family, and let them know I would not be coming for the Christmas holidays, due to my job.

Anyway, God was surely working in my life and He knew what He was doing. As I look back to my not being able to go to Pittsburgh at that time, I know it was for the best. If I would have gone to visit my family that Christmas,

I probably would not have gone back to Georgia. At the time, I was pretty vulnerable. I believe that I would have fallen prey to the control of the woman I had worked for, feel sorry for her, and end up staying in Pittsburgh. After all, to return to the restaurant business that I knew very well would have been the easy thing to do. I would be in my comfort zone. And most definitely, this would not have been good for me. God did see to it that the financial situation was worked out. And, I did take my finals that semester, and return for the spring semester. The spring semester began. I was disappointed that I only made a 2.5 GPA, and not the 4.0 GPA that I wanted for the fall semester. A 2.5 GPA was enough to be able to declare a major. So, I applied to declare a major in psychology. Things were going okay, and I was still writing to Dr. M. regarding my abuse issues.

In February of 2005, I finally got the courage to schedule an appointment with the campus counselor to deal with my abuse issues. I had never been to any counselor in my life, but I felt it was now time to take the challenge of dealing with my past. I thought, "How hard could this be?" Now, I knew the details of my abuse by heart, having replayed them in my mind over and over again. So, my idea of a counseling session was just this; I would go to the counselor, tell her what happened to me, talk about it a few times, and I mean only a few times, and that's it; it's over. I'm better. Just think, I was studying to be a counselor. Needless to say, I was in for a rude awakening. When I went to my first counseling appointment, I had to fill out paperwork about my family history. I left a lot of blanks on the paperwork, because I really did not know much about my family history. I completed the paperwork, and it was time for me to talk to the counselor. I dressed myself in my defensive attire, attitude and all, and was ready to take on the counselor. I walked into the counselor's office, and she introduced herself to me. I will call the counselor Ms. H. I sat down. Ms. H. was going over the paperwork and asking me questions about it. I gave an awful lot of "I don't knows" to her questions, because I truly did not know. After Ms. H. finished going over the paperwork, she asked me if I could tell her what happened to me. If I remember correctly, I gave her a quick yes, I can. What happened to me next would be the most traumatizing pain ever. I was starting to tell her my story when in my right ear I could hear heavy breathing and panting. The sound was horrific. I could hear Ms. H. asking me if I could tell her what was happening, but I could not. I remember holding my hands onto my ears telling the breathing to stop. Ms. H. was still trying to get me to tell her what was happening. I remember telling her, "No, I can't, I can't." At that moment, I felt my life had been taken from me. I did not know what was happening to me, and at the time I do not think Ms. H. knew what was happening either. The breathing sound finally subsided. I do not think I was able to say anymore or talk about what had happened to me. Ms. H. asked me if I was okay, and I am sure that I said yes. We wrapped up the session, and I left. I got into my car, and drove to a lake that I went to frequently. I was crying uncontrollably the whole time. I was devastated by what I had experienced. I wanted to crawl into the deepest, darkest hole on the face of the earth and die. I got to the lake, went to what was called The Broken Bridges, turned around, and headed back toward the highway. There was a boat ramp at the lake where you back your boat down into the water. As I drove toward the ramp, in my mind I could visualize me and my car in the water, slowly sinking. I wanted to drive right into the water. I had both hands on the steering wheel, but the wheel would not turn to go down the ramp. I kept going straight past the boat ramp and out toward the highway. I knew for sure that it was God who took the wheel steering my car that day. He still had a plan for me and dying was not it. I did not tell anyone what I was going through that day. I got myself back together and did the things I had to do.

I had another appointment scheduled with the counselor for the following week. It took me a whole week to regain my strength from the trauma. I went back for my appointment with the counselor. This time, I was able to tell about my abuse and explain what had happened to me in her office the previous week. I believe I told Ms. H. what happened to me was like a nightmare. I remember she joked and said it was more like a "daymare," because it was daytime when it happened. But, in reality it was a horrifying flashback. At the time, I do not think I even knew or comprehended what a flashback was. For those of you who may not know what a flashback is, it is reliving the traumatic event as if it were happening in the present. That flashback stripped me of my life that day, figuratively speaking. In an instant, my mind was traveling fast to reach the memories that were treading my soul. I could not believe that I could experience such trauma just talking about my abuse; after all, I knew what happened to me by heart, and it should not have affected me. But, I think what happened to me now was that the abuse became real to me. It was no longer just in my head; it was in my heart now. The reality was that the abuse was about me. The days that would follow that first counseling session would be significantly challenging for me. I had let Ms. H. know that when I left her office the week before, I really considered taking my life by driving my car into the lake. She asked me why I did not tell her about wanting to hurt myself before our visit that day. I simply told her that it was not important. But, I know that maybe I felt that I was not important; I did not matter, and no one would care anyway. Ms. H. discussed with me a safety plan and asked me to sign a contract to not harm myself before our next visit. I agreed to the contract, and I signed it. That first flashback was only the beginning of what was to come, but God had begun the healing process in me.

I was now seeing Ms. H. on a regular basis once a week. As the semester continued, strange things were happening to me One day, I was heading to class, and I had seen one of my professors driving by. The weather was still cold, and I had a coat on. I remember as she was passing by in her car, I waved to her. Then, as she passed me by, I took my coat and wrapped it around me as tight as I could. That day, I remember feeling such shame. I felt like I was naked; everyone could see me, and I was wearing a sign on me that told what had happened to me, that I was raped. That day I felt like the whole world knew now.

Academically, school was very, very, challenging. My memory was failing me. I was forgetting basic day to day things or things I needed to know. This was tremendously difficult for me to accept, because I felt that God had gifted me with an excellent memory. I was always able to remember just about everything I had ever done. Sometimes, you might have to give me a few minutes to remember, but I could remember. I relied very much on my memory. Studying for tests was extremely difficult, due to my failing memory. One of my classes required me to memorize a host of different countries and be able to name them on a blank map for a test. I was not able to do this. I ended up failing the class. I was bewildered as to what was happening to my memory.

I enjoyed my job at Wal-Mart. I felt that I was very good at being a cashier, but I was getting very irritated with everyone and everything, although no one knew this. On the days I had to work, after about two hours of working, I felt ready to slap people for no apparent reason. I was so touchy and filled with anxiety. I could not even stand myself, and I was getting on my own nerves. Still, I could not understand why I was so miserable or what was happening to me.

The flashbacks continued, and they were very powerful. They were like a raging undercurrent just swirling around the memories in my head, just waiting to suck me in. The flashbacks were triggered by things such as watching a movie on television, a noise, or just nothing at all. The flashbacks took all my strength and energy. When I had one, they drained me both physically and emotionally. Flashbacks were not something I would even wish on my worst enemy. The flashbacks came pretty consistently now, were severe, and appeared at any time of the day. I could be driving down the road or just about to fall asleep, and suddenly I would have another flashback. It was like watching reruns of a horror show on television. And some parts of my rapes I could see very clearly during the flashbacks, just as if I were there. I was that little girl reliving the very details of my abuse all over again. At some point, the flashbacks came more frequently at night, just when I would fall asleep. The painful memories I locked in my heart so long ago, were now invading my perfect world where no one could hurt me. One night, just as I drifted off to sleep, clearly I could hear the sounds of a little girl crying off in the distance. In my sleep, I could see the little girl in her blue dress sitting on the floor with clothes underneath her, her knees clinched tightly to her chest, arms around her knees, and her head placed down on her knees, just crying. That little girl was me, and the flashback was a memory of my first rape. Many nights I cried myself to sleep. I felt like I was all alone. No one could ever understand what was happening to me. During these times, I felt I had no one I could turn to, no one I could see physically, no one that could just comfort and hold me when the flashbacks came, and tell me everything was going to be okay. It was just God and I. My tears were never ending. There was a song that I remember that I think was called "Cry Me a River." Well, forget about the river; I cried me an ocean. During this time, I memorized a Bible verse, Isaiah 41:10, which says; "Do not fear for I am with you: do not anxiously look about you, for I am your God. I will strengthen you, surely I will help you, surely I will uphold you with my righteous right hand." So many nights, this verse was all I had to comfort my soul, and I would repeat this verse over and over again until I fell fast asleep.

That spring semester was quickly coming to a close. Physically, I felt nauseated everyday, just wanting to vomit for no reason. Over the years, I had bought a lot of beautiful jewelry, such as gold necklaces, earrings, and rings. At this time, being a woman was something that I think I subconsciously wanted to forget. I started giving all my jewelry away, because I didn't want to wear it anymore. No longer did I enjoy wearing perfume and eye shadow. I gave all my perfume away. Anything that was a reminder of my being a woman was something I did not want to have anything to do with. There were times during my therapy that I felt responsible for what happened to me and that I caused these people to rape me.

Driving was becoming a challenge for me. I was not able to remember driving to and from school. One day, I pulled up in the driveway where I lived. Literally, I could not remember driving home from school. I did not remember stopping at lights, stop signs, driving through town or anything. Another time, I was driving down my road toward school. I was obviously off in another world, because before I knew it I was heading into the opposite lane, and almost crashed into a person that happened to be someone I worked with at Wal-Mart. He swerved to avoid hitting me. This was a reality check. Then, I really knew something was desperately wrong with me.

After the semester ended, I believe it was at this time that my counselor told me that she felt I was depressed enough to consider taking medication. Well, I remember when she told me I was depressed, I was devastated. I had no idea that this was what was wrong with me. To find out that I was depressed was such a shock to me, but a good explanation as to what was happening to me and how I felt. I remember thinking in my head, oh no, my ex-boss could never know about this, because she said I was crazy, and this would only confirm her thoughts about me. I guess to me depression equaled being crazy. At this time, I am sure that I did not completely comprehend what being depressed really meant. My counselor and I discussed depression, taking medication for it, and the length of time I would have to take the medication for it to be effective. She told me that she did not mention taking depression medication sooner, because I had expressed to her before that I did not like taking medication for any reason. She was right. I hated taking medication for anything. My counselor suggested that I consider the possibility of taking depression medication and let her know my decision in our next session. At this time, I did not inform any of my family members as to what I was going through.

At my next counseling session, I told my counselor if she really felt I needed medication for depression, I would agree to take it. Her secretary called the clinic in town, and made a doctor's appointment for me. I went to the doctor's office, and he put me on medication for depression. I continued my counseling sessions over the summer.

For part of my therapy, my counselor recommended that I keep a journal about my thoughts and feelings. I was reluctant, because I did not like writing my feelings on a piece of paper. Anyway, with my limited vocabulary, it was difficult to express my feelings verbally. When my counselor would ask me how I was feeling, I remember my primary word to her was that I felt sad. Eventually, my feeling vocabulary grew to anger. Sad and angry were my basic feelings in my early days of counseling, because I did not know any other words to describe how I felt. My counselor gave me a word list of feelings to help me to describe what I felt. Of course, there were quite a few words I had never heard of or known the meaning of, but I did learn some of them. I did keep a journal for therapeutic purposes which did prove to be very helpful. Ms. H. suggested some books to read about sexual abuse. If I remember correctly, the first book I read about sexual abuse was *The Wounded Heart* by Dan B. Allender. I remember it took me probably about a month or more just to finish the first chapter. The contents of the book were hard for me to digest. I continued to read more books about survivors of sexual abuse. These books helped me to know that I was not the only one out there who had gone through sexual abuse.

Things were not going well with the two ladies with whom I was sharing an apartment. I felt like they were teaming up against me, treating me as if I were nothing. For instance, sometime after I had moved into the apartment, Jody and the other girl got together to decide how to divide up the household chores. They made all the decisions without including me. If they were having a conversation they would stop talking when I was around. My intuition was telling me something was wrong, and they were up to something. I discussed the situation with my counselor, but I could not give her specific information as to what was happening. I think maybe my counselor probably thought I was paranoid or something, because I am sure it appeared that way. It was very difficult to specifically state what I felt the girls were doing to me, because I could not explain it and I had no proof. Thinking back to that time, I remember Jody telling me one time something to the effect that she was afraid the other girl that shared our apartment with us would like me more as a friend than her. To be honest, I really did not care who was better friends with whom. One day, Jody told me that she and the other girl thought that I was a criminal. I could not believe that they would accuse me of being a criminal, because they had no just cause. Anyway, I was not a criminal. I felt that maybe Jody was trying to turn the other girl against me. Then, I began to notice that mutual friends that Jody and I had shared were treating me differently. Some of our mutual friends would not speak to me or were cold toward me when I would see them. At this time, I really did not know what the problem was with the girls with whom I shared the apartment. In spite of the stressful situation, I still liked these girls as friends.

At the end of the spring semester of 1995, one of the girls that shared our apartment moved out. Then, in December of 1995 Jody moved out of the apartment. After the spring semester of 1996, Jody withdrew from college and moved to another city. Shortly after Jody had left the college, I was talking with a lady that worked on campus one day. The lady proceeded to inform me that Jody was telling her all kinds of things about me, and she wanted to tell me what Jody had told her. At that point, I interrupted her and said that I did not want to know what Jody said about me. I felt that if this lady did not tell me what Jody was saying about me while Jody was there, then I did not want to know now. I was pretty sure that Jody was making up lies about me. Also, one day I had gone to work, and one of my co-workers proceeded to inform me that Jody had said things about me at my job. I simply told that person that if she wanted to believe whatever it was that Jody told her then she could believe it, because again I did not want to know what Jody said. I had prayed many times to the Lord that He would let me know the truth about my life. My intuition did not fail me. God now confirmed to me that my feelings were right about Jody, and that she was trying to turn people against me.

That summer of 1995, I let my brother Drew and my sister Charity know about my abuse, and that I was now suffering with severe depression. I am sure the news was a shock to them, but I was now ready to let someone know what was happening to me. I felt I could trust Drew and Charity with this information about me. After six months of pretty severe flashbacks, they were beginning to slow down. Also, I figured out that the flashbacks came from the left side of my brain, because I would usually have the flashbacks when

I would turn my head directly to the left. Knowing this about the flashbacks, would allow me to have some control over them. Diligently, I continued to go to counseling sessions and work on my issues. As difficult as it was for me to go to sessions every week, I desired to get better. I knew that God would give me the strength and courage to get better. God was working, but slowly, I felt. I met a young lady, whom I will call Beth who had been sexually abused. We became friends, and it was good to talk to someone that I could relate to about what I was going through. One day while Beth and I were talking, I was disillusioned, and still under the impression that this was all going to go away. She said that my abuse will always be part of me and who I am. Well, this was a shock to me and my unrealistic idea that somehow I still thought this would all go away. When Beth told me this, I cried uncontrollably. I guess I thought I could wash the abuse all away as if nothing ever happened.

Sometime in March of 1996, in a letter, I confronted my family member that raped me. I let him know that I knew what he did to me. Also, I sent a letter to my mother to tell her about what happened to me. My family member called me to deny that he did anything to me, and he expressed that he was more concerned about how my mother took the news about me. I never heard from my mother. After my confrontation, I only talked to a few of my family.

As for the woman I worked for for fourteen years, she was trying to contact me through my family and letters. She wanted me to come back to work for her. Funny, because in a letter she wrote to me sometime shortly after I came to Georgia, she told me that I was evil, and I needed help. Now, she wanted me back. In August of 1996, my ex-boss sent me a certified letter. I do not think I had ever received a certified letter in my life. I remember going to the post office on campus to get my mail. I got a note from the postal clerk that I had to come to the desk and pick up a letter I had to sign for, or something to that effect. I had been waiting for something from my sister Charity, and I thought that this was from her. I walked into the post office to get the certified letter. The postal clerk handed me the letter and showed me where to sign. When I looked at the envelope, I knew the letter was not from my sister, because I was expecting a package from her. I looked at the sender's name. It was from my ex-boss. Inside, I froze, and placed the letter back down on the counter. My intuition was telling me that there was money in the envelope. And if there was money in the envelope, it was the devil's money. It was just a way for my ex-boss to have control over me. The postal clerk looked at me, and said that I did not have to sign for the letter, and that I could send it back. At that moment, God brought to my mind the verse in I Corinthians 10:13 which talks about being overtaken by temptation and how God will provide a way out of temptation. This was definitely a temptation. Considering my financial situation, I really could have used that money. I never opened the letter. Instead, I slid the letter back across the counter to the clerk. God gave me perfect peace with my decision to not accept the letter. He had provided a way out for me, an option I was not aware of that I had. I knew that if I accepted that money, I would have paid for that wrong choice. A few weeks later in a phone conversation with my sister Charity, she told me that she had seen my ex-boss. My ex-boss told my sister that she had sent me a lot of money, and I sent it back to her. Again, God let me know my intuition was right. He was protecting me not only against the wiles of temptation, but from the control of my ex-boss. I know God wanted me to trust Him to provide for me, and this was not from Him. On a visit back to Pittsburgh quite some time ago, I visited a friend of mine that worked with me at the Hoagie shop. She informed me that my ex-boss told her that I had stolen a lot of money from her. My friend said she didn't believe her, because she knew it was a lie. I thanked my friend for not believing her, because it was not true. My heart was saddened about what my ex-boss told her and maybe more people, but I couldn't do anything about it.

Being a full-time student, working full-time and working on my abuse issues full-time was taking its toll on me physically, emotionally, and academically. After the end of the spring semester of 1996, I was put on academic probation for the fall semester of 1996, due to a grade point average which was a 1.469. And that summer I was diagnosed with asthma. Let me mention here, that I had no medical insurance at this time. Prior to this, I considered myself to be a physically healthy person with no major health problems, except a weight problem that was increasing. It was hard to maintain a forty-hour-a-week job, school, and counseling sessions. I was having difficulty at Wal-Mart working around my school schedule. So, I looked for another job. I got hired at a Christian book store. It didn't last long. About two weeks later, I was fired. The manager said that I was not going to work out. Things were looking pretty dark at this time. Sometime in May of 1996, I got word that my nephew Paul was missing, and his girlfriend was dead. In June of 1996, I got news that Paul was found dead. I was devastated. Paul was like my child, and I was not able to go to Pittsburgh to attend the funeral services. To this day my family still does not know the circumstances surrounding my nephew and his girlfriend's death. Losing my job, things were financially challenging, and I had no savings. I only worked to meet my basic needs. I had to do something. So, I wrote to my brother Ed to ask him if he could lend me some money. Ed lent me five hundred dollars to make it through the month. My sister Charity was my own Red Cross angel. She sent me food, school supplies, clothing, and other miscellaneous supplies, not only during my desperate days, but still today. Charity

and Ed never knew how much I appreciated their willing-
ness to help in a desperate time of need.

My landlord was manager at the gift shop on campus,
and she offered me a job. I accepted her offer. In order to do
better at school, I had to cut my work hours down to twenty
hours a week, during the school semester, but this would
not be enough to cover my living expenses. So, I applied
for the maximum amount of financial aid to cover my living
expenses. I was able to do this for the rest of my time in
college. My job working at the gift shop was much less
stressful and more workable than the previous job.

Being on academic probation that fall meant that I was
not allowed to take more than twelve hours of classes. Also,
if I did not achieve a 2.0 GPA or better that semester, then
I would not be able to take classes for the spring semester.
This would not be good for me. Well, I had already signed
up for fourteen class hours that semester. I really needed the
extra class that I was scheduled for, because if I remember
correctly the class was only offered that semester. I had to
make an appeal to the Academic Dean to permit me to take
the fourteen class hours that I was scheduled for. I got a tutor
for any classes that I was having difficulty with. The college
provided tutors free of charge. That was such a blessing for
me. I did a lot of praying that semester, and I know a lot of
people who were praying for me. The fall semester came
to an end. I was able to take the fourteen hours of classes
I signed up for. I ended the semester with a 3.150 GPA.
What a difference from the 1.469 GPA the semester before!
I was no longer on academic probation. Yea! What praise
to God! In Jeremiah 33:3 it says: "Call to me, and I will
answer you, I will tell you great and mighty things, which
you do not know." God certainly empowered me with His
wisdom and knowledge. I called upon the Lord, and He was
faithful to answer my prayers, especially academically. He
was taking great care of me, and supplying my every need.

I truly received an abundance of God's grace and favor that semester. God exceeded my prayer requests.

My days at Toccoa Falls College were quickly coming to a close. I still continued to work on my abuse issues and receive counseling services. In January of 1998, I wanted to give testimony to all that God had done, and was doing, in my life up to this point. In your last semester at Toccoa Falls College, you were able to sign up to give a senior testimony in chapel. So, I signed up to do my testimony. There were a lot of people signed up to do a senior testimony and only a limited amount of slots. I was not sure that I would be selected to give my senior testimony. Some time went by and I got word that I had been selected to give my testimony in chapel on March 20, 1998. I was so excited, but nervous. There was not much time for me to prepare. So, I had to get to work. Who would have ever dreamed that I would be speaking to a large crowd of people telling them all that the Lord had done for me. I was absolutely not a speaker. For example, the college required all students to take a class in public speaking. The class required you to do several different types of speeches. The speeches were graded by the teacher and your classmates. Well, I remember dreading taking this class, because I was terrified to have to talk about myself in front of a lot of people. I had a couple of friends who were taking the class with me. We got together to discuss what we were doing for our speeches. I really had no clue as to how to give a speech. The worst part of this class was that you had to speak proper grammar. Oh, this was a huge challenge for me! It was very difficult to try to make sure I spoke properly. Anyway, one day my friends and I were discussing our upcoming Hall of Fame speech. In this speech, you told about someone that you admired, and told why he/she should be voted into the Hall of Fame. I decided to vote my best friend Sandy into the Hall of Fame. My friends and I were discussing introductions for our speeches. I said that I could do a cheer, since Sandy and I were cheerleaders together. My friends said that doing a cheer would be really good, and I trusted their opinions. I was really excited, plus I wanted to get a good grade. The day finally came for me to do my Hall of Fame speech. I did my cheer as planned, and the class got a big kick out of this. I was so nervous. I had to keep my composure so I could complete my speech. After class, my friends said they couldn't believe I did a cheer. On of my friends, Sherry asked me if I didn't see her rolling on the floor laughing. I told her no. Then I said that she told me to do the cheer. Sherry said, "I didn't think you would take me seriously, and actually do it." Anyway, recalling that time, I thought the cheer was a great attention getter. I did not do very well in speech class. I think my final grade was a "D," but it was definitely an experience I will not forget.

Now, I was going to embark on a huge speaking engagement talking about my life, my senior testimony. I planned to sing a Christian song called, "Jesus Will Still Be There," recorded by the group Point of Grace at the end of my testimony. I was not a singer, but I loved to sing. I asked a friend of mine, who was a singer, if she would sing with me and she said yes. Then, I asked Sherry and a couple other friends if they would introduce me. My friend Tracey would lead in praise and worship with a few worship songs. Things were coming together. I was still so nervous, but God gave me peace about doing my testimony. The big day was finally here, March 20, 1998, and it was the first day of spring. We had had some bad weather and rain the day before. A tornado had touched down in a city about forty-five minutes away from where I was, and it was still raining a little. Chapel didn't start until 10:00 a.m. I had some time before chapel. I remember driving around that morning praying for the rain to go away and that it would be a beautiful day. I prayed that God would be with me as I spoke in chapel, and that whoever He needed to be in chapel would be there. Also,

I prayed that God would bless my voice, and sing through my heart, and touch whomever's heart needed to be touched that day. Senior testimonies were usually given in Friday Chapel and were not well attended. But much to my surprise, chapel was pretty full this day. There were around a few hundred faculty, staff, and students in attendance. Outside, the rain had stopped, and the sun had broken through the clouds and was shining brightly. I had only really practiced my speech completely a couple of times on the Wednesday night prior to my Friday morning speaking engagement. You should have seen the testimony I had written to read from. It was about eight pages long. In Chapel, Tracey had already finished praise and worship, and Sherry and my other friends were just finishing up introducing me. After my friends had finished praise and worship and the introduction, I only had thirty minutes to speak. Now it was time for me to speak. My asthma was not cooperating with me that day, so I had to bring some drinking water, just in case. Feeling a little bit of anxiety, but having God's perfect peace, I got up to speak. Usually, it was not quiet in chapel. Some people were carrying on conversations, doing homework, studying for tests, and you could hear paper rustling around.

For my introduction, I told about speech class and how terrified I was to speak. Then I sang a brief chorus from a song called, "Don't Rain on My Parade," recorded by Barbara Streisand. After I finished singing, there was complete silence. It was so silent you could hear a pin drop. I got a little emotional during my speech, but I made it through. I really did not recall reading from my notes at all, and I do not believe I really did with the exception of finding a reference to a verse that I wanted to quote. My friend came up with me to sing my song. The song was over, and I began gathering my things. The audience usually clapped for whoever was speaking. As I looked up from gathering my things, not only was the audience clapping, but I got a standing ovation. It was a true honor. Some people were crying, coming over to me, hugging me, and complimenting my singing. I was so elated that I could not even cry. That day was filled with God's glory. The Holy Spirit spoke through my heart, and in that chapel you truly could sense the presence of the Holy Spirit. The joy that was in my heart was overwhelming. What an amazing day the Lord blessed me with, and there was more to come!

Maybe here I could certainly relate to Moses when God asked him to go to speak to Pharaoh. Moses was afraid, because he said he could not speak well. In Exodus 4:10-12 it says: "But Moses pleaded with the Lord, "Oh Lord, I'm just not a good speaker. I never have been, and I'm not now, even after you have spoken to me, I'm clumsy with words." "Who makes mouths?" the Lord asked him. "Who makes people so they can speak or not speak, hear or not hear, see or not see? Is it not I, the Lord? Now go, and do as I have told you. I will help you speak well, and I will tell you what to say." I was afraid, but I did what I felt the Lord asked me to do. And He did empower me with the words to speak in chapel.

After chapel that day, I left the campus, because I did not have classes. Later that day, I returned to campus to pick up my mail and drop off a report that I had to turn in. When I got to campus, Tracey and Sherry came running over to me saying you won't believe what happened. I got scared thinking something tragic happened, but Tracey said people have been coming up to her telling her about my testimony and how great it was. I remember Sherry commented saying, "No one gets a standing ovation in chapel, and you did," I was at a loss for words, because of what God had done.

Faculty, staff, and students continued to make comments to me about what an impact I made in giving my testimony. One professor said that some of her students were talking about my testimony in her class. She commented that one of the students was a young man. She said it was unusual for her to hear a young man commenting on a testimony. I could not believe it. I had seen one of my professors the following week. I recall my professor saying to me, "Did you not know you could speak?" Looking at her with surprise I said, how would I know that? I told her that I just did what I felt God wanted me to do. Being obedient to God in this situation paid such great dividends. I guess I did learn something in speech class after all. Then, my professor proceeded to tell me that she heard students all over campus singing the song I sang. I remember telling her that that is how I knew that God touched someone's heart with the song, just as I had prayed. God says in His word in Ephesians 3:20: "Now to Him who is able to do exceeding abundantly beyond all that we ask or think, according to the power that works within us," and no doubt, God far exceeded my expectations that day. It was a glorious day!

Graduation was getting closer, and I wanted to get my Master's Degree in counseling, so I could get my professional license. I knew my cumulative grade point average was not high, so I would be limited as to where I could apply for a Master's Degree. Also, I wanted to stay in this area. I checked into the counseling program at Clemson University in South Carolina. They had a Master's program in counseling that I was interested in. I met with the director in the counseling department. He told me that it would be best if I waited until I completed my schooling at Toccoa Falls College before I apply to Clemson. I believe I had to have no less than a 2.7 cumulative grade point average. Taking the Graduate Record Examinations (GRE) was a requirement for entrance into the Master's program, but if I had a 3.6 cumulative grade point average over my last four semesters at Toccoa Falls College, then the GRE would be waived.

On May 9, 1998, I graduated from Toccoa Falls College. I had a double major and my degree would be in both psychology and counseling skills. My overall cumulative grade point average was a 2.767, which was good enough to apply at Clemson University. And I had made at least a 3.6 cumulative grade point average over my last four semesters. I was exempt from taking the GRE. I think I even made the Dean's list a couple of times in my last four semesters. I could not believe all that God had done for me.

After I graduated, I immediately applied at Clemson University for their Community Agency Counseling Program. Also, I applied for the assistantship program to work on campus at Clemson University. Everyone that applied to Clemson was eligible for an assistantship. Getting an assistantship would also provide lower tuition.

The second week in June of 1998, I got very sick. I had severe stomach pain, dry heaves, and was very nauseated. The pain was great. My doctor's office was already closed. So, I went to the emergency room at the hospital to get checked out by a doctor. This was a serious decision for me, because as I said earlier, I did not have medical insurance. I would have to come up with the money to pay for the visit. I believe it was on a Friday night that I had gone to the emergency room. I believe the doctor suspected a gall bladder problem, possibly stones. The emergency room doctor told me to go to my primary doctor, and he would order a sonogram to check for gallstones. Well, I thought this was ridiculous. This doctor wanted me to go to my primary doctor only for him to send me right back down there to the hospital. This emergency room doctor could actually order the sonogram right then. So, being the persistent person I am, I gave my argument as to why this emergency room doctor should just order the sonogram to check for gallstones for me right then; I insisted that he do just that. I was able to get an appointment for a sonogram the very next morning. The sonogram showed no signs of gallstones. I was told to schedule an appointment with my primary doctor the following week, and I did.

When I went for my doctor's appointment, I told him the symptoms I was having. My doctor suspected gall bladder problems. I think he may have given me some medication and sent me on my way. I continued to be sick, and I think I was having difficulty eating. My eating habits changed drastically, which was a good thing. No more drive through fast food service for me anymore. I returned to the doctor at the beginning of July, 1998. My doctor ordered an x-ray, and I was diagnosed with severe acid reflux. He prescribed medication for me and scheduled a follow-up appointment. I was losing weight rapidly, because it was difficult for me to eat. When all was said and done, I lost about one hundred pounds in about eight months. At the follow-up appointment, I continued to have the same symptoms (i.e. stomach pain and nausea). My doctor then ordered an x-ray to check for gallstones. Prior to the test, I had to take a lot of medication. The day I had the x-ray, the x-ray technician asked me if I had taken all the medication, and I said yes. Then she asked me if I had already had my gall bladder removed, and I told her no. The x-ray technician could not find my gall bladder. I went to see my doctor. My doctor reviewed my x-rays. He felt I had an enlarged gall bladder and referred me to a local surgeon. My surgeon reviewed my records, and I told her the problems I was having. My surgeon performed all the tests possible with my gall bladder. At the time, my surgeon said that she was ninety-nine percent sure that my gall bladder was not the problem. I continued on medication for acid reflux, and I continued to be sick.

In August, my job at Toccoa Falls College would end, because I would no longer be a student there. I would then be in need of a job. Some time in July of 1998, I received word that I had been accepted at Clemson University for the fall semester. I had to go to Clemson to meet with my advisor and sign up for classes. On the day I arrived on campus to sign up for classes, I was walking down the hall in the education building, and no one was anywhere to be found. Then, a woman came walking down the hall toward me. She stopped and asked me if she could help me. I told her no thanks and said that I was there to sign up for classes, and I knew where I needed to go. Then, I said something to the effect of how hard was it to get an assistantship? Just from the way she looked at me, I said, "Pretty hard, huh?" She then informed me that on the fourth floor in the education department there were some openings for assistantships. The lady told me where to go, and with whom to speak. I proceeded to the third floor where I met with the director of the counseling department to sign up for classes. I made my schedule for classes. I inquired of him if there were any job openings in the counseling department. The director said there weren't, because all his student workers were scheduled to return in the fall. I got on the elevator and pushed the button to go to the first floor to head home. I decided that I was not going to stop on the fourth floor to check out the job opportunities there. I would do it another day. I got to the first floor and just as the elevator door was opening something made me stop and decide to push the button to go to the fourth floor. When I got to the fourth floor, I was able to get an interview with the director in the education department. I let him know that I was pursuing an assistantship at Clemson. He told me he was in need of some workers and that I needed to bring him a resume. Immediately, I went back to my house in Georgia, got a resume and returned it to the director of the education department. The director said that he would let me know about a job in a couple of weeks. A couple of weeks went by, and I had not heard from the director at Clemson. School would be starting soon, and my job at Toccoa Falls College was almost over. I was in need of a job. I called the director of education at Clemson, inquired about the possibility of my getting a job there. The director said that he was going to hire me and gave me instruction as to what I needed to do next. God was right there directing my every step and making sure I did not go off in my own direction. One of my favorite verses in the Bible is in Proverbs 3:5-6. It says: "Trust in the Lord with all your heart, and do not lean on your own understanding. In all your ways acknowledge Him, and He will make your paths straight." When I wanted to turn around and head home that day, and not pursue the job at the time, God redirected my steps to make sure I did what He needed me to do.

I was physically sick, having the same symptoms, and under a doctor's care. My doctor still felt that my gall bladder was the problem, but my surgeon and all the tests disagreed. I would enter my Master's program physically sick. School finally started. I was a full-time graduate student and working part-time. I commuted from my home in Georgia to Clemson University in South Carolina every day, except Friday. I did not have classes that day. It was about a thirty to forty minute ride one way. I knew this would be an adjustment. My job at Clemson was great. I loved the people I worked with and the opportunity I had here. Again, God had blessed me with some wonderful teachers and people to work with.

Academically, school was still very challenging for me. The standard requirements for my Master's program required that you were only allowed to make two "C's" throughout the whole two-year program. The pressure was on, but the academic training at Toccoa Falls College had prepared me well for my new challenge. Now, I was facing some great anxiety to perform academically.

I got adjusted to my school and to my work schedule. I continued to be sick. In December of 1998, my primary doctor suggested that I go for a second opinion about my gall bladder. I did. The surgeon that I had seen for my second opinion diagnosed me with gall bladder disease. I told that surgeon to forward the results of his diagnosis back to my primary doctor, because I did not want him to perform my surgery. I called my primary doctor to tell him that I wanted the surgeon I had gone to first to perform my surgery. My doctor said that he would call my surgeon, and see if she would agree to perform gall bladder surgery on me, considering my continuing symptoms and the new report.

On January 5, 1999, I had gall bladder surgery. After surgery, I remember my surgeon coming into the hospital room and telling me all the tests lied. She said as soon as she opened me up, she knew it was my gall bladder. She said the stones were popping out, and there was scar tissue, which meant the stones had been popping out all along. I guess technology is not always right. My surgery was a little traumatic for me, due to my abuse issues. I was feeling very vulnerable. Also, my surgeon was a woman, and I had never had a woman doctor, nor would I have chosen one before. Not choosing a woman doctor was probably due to the fact that I have had a male doctor all of my life, because there were not a lot of women doctors around when I was young. Anyway, my surgeon was absolutely wonderful. God even provided some emotional healing through my surgeon. This surgery would be the first of six surgeries during my Master's program.

I was still attending school at Clemson. If my memory serves me right, school started the same day as my surgery. I was not really able to miss classes, and two days after my surgery I returned to school. When I returned to my surgeon for my follow-up appointment, I could not thank her enough. I felt great. My surgeon told me that I was atypical, because of what she considered my unusual symptoms for a gall bladder patient. My surgeon did some exploratory surgery at the time she did my gall bladder, and she told me that she found a hernia located in the right groin area. To be a woman and have a hernia in this area was not typical. I asked my surgeon what I needed to do. She told me nothing, unless the hernia started causing me problems. Then, on my merry way I went.

Sometime in February of 1999, I began having shooting pains down my right leg and abdominal pain in the area where the hernia was located. I was pretty sure that my hernia was causing a problem. I went on the internet to find information about the symptoms of a hernia problem. The information pretty much described my symptoms. At this time, I was having some abnormal vaginal bleeding. I checked out a few other avenues to make sure I did not have some type of infection or other problem, and I didn't. I called my surgeon to schedule an appointment to see her. When I went to my appointment, I told my surgeon the symptoms I was having. I told her I felt that the hernia was causing the problem. So, she said, "Let's fix it." Spring break was coming up shortly in March, so I scheduled my hernia surgery for then.

I had spent four years in counseling services working on my abuse issues, with the first two years being the most intensive. God had done some amazing emotional healing. I had taken the depression medication for only thirteen months, and that was it. I felt the depression had passed, and I did not need the medication anymore. There are not enough words to express my thanks to God for His provision of a most awesome counselor during my time of need. And I thank God that Toccoa Falls College provided the services free of charge, because I could have never paid for those intensive services. Even though I knew what happened to me, I was now searching for some physical evidence that I was raped. I know that I could not have had the flashbacks, if I had not been raped, but I still wanted physical proof. For whatever reason, I guess part of me now started to doubt these events ever happened to me.

Somewhere between my first and second surgery, I had a scheduled appointment to see my gynecologist for a routine check-up. At this time, I informed my gynecologist that I had been raped as a child, and that I wanted to know if there was any physical evidence. My gynecologist did his exam. But there was no proof I was raped. My doctor said that everything was in tact. My doctor said I was a virgin, and he said he would have never known I was raped. I remember getting angry and saying that I was raped. My doctor made sure that I was alright and asked me if I was receiving help. I told him that I had received help, and then I left his office. My hernia surgery came and went. My surgeon told me that I had the biggest hernia that she had ever seen in someone so young. It was that atypical thing again.

The abnormal vaginal bleeding continued, and I called my gynecologist. The day I called the doctor's office, my doctor was not in, and I turned down being seen by his partner. The bleeding continued and again I called the doctor's office to see if I could get an appointment. The receptionist gave me a time and told me to come in that day. I went to my gynecologist's office, assuming he was there to see me. Much to my surprise my doctor's partner, Dr. R., would see me for my appointment. I went in for my exam. I explained to Dr. R. the problems I was having. I also told him that I had been raped as a child and was looking for physical evidence that this had happened to me. Dr. R. examined me. I was in much pain and had never had anything like this before. After the examination, Dr. R. came in to talk to me. He was not really sure what was wrong with me. Dr. R. said that he thought that I had something called vestibulitis. I had never heard of such a thing. Dr. R. said that he wanted to try some medication to see if this would correct the problem. If the medication did not work, then we would talk about surgery to remove a gland located in the vaginal wall. I asked Dr. R. if he could tell that I had been raped. Dr. R.'s conclusion was the same as my regular gynecologist. I was still a virgin, and there was no physical proof that I had been raped. I kept praying to God to show me the truth.

Needless to say, the medication did not work, and I was still in much pain. I called Dr. R.'s office to schedule another appointment. Dr. R. wanted to do a biopsy in his office. I went for my appointment and examination. Dr. R. said that he would not do the biopsy, because it would have caused me more pain. At some point, Dr. R. decided that he would do exploratory surgery and remove the gland. I had a break that summer between school sessions, so I scheduled the surgery for June of 1999.

My surgery came and went. I went back to see Dr. R. for a follow-up appointment. I was feeling great. I told Dr. R. that I highly recommended this surgery, if someone needed to have it. Dr. R. had done a biopsy when he did my surgery. What Dr. R. would tell me next would be devastating. Dr. R. said that my biopsy came back, and I tested positive for the Human Papilloma Virus (HPV), a sexually transmitted disease (STD). Bewildered, I asked Dr. R. what this meant to my life. Dr. R. explained the disease to me and said there is no other way to get this disease, but through sexual contact. Dr. R. told me that he knew a couple that had the Human Papilloma Virus, and they were doing okay. He said they didn't appear to be having any problems. Also, having HPV puts me at a greater risk for cervical cancer and there is no known cure for HPV. Dr. R. just suggested that if I got married to let my partner know that I had HPV. Shocked, I was completely ravaged by this news and what having this STD would mean to my life. However, God did answer my prayers, and now I had physical proof that I had been raped. No longer did I have to doubt all the horrific memories, because now I knew the whole truth.

The medical bills were mounting; I was still suffering with asthma. I was struggling financially. I was able to apply for indigent care to cover the cost of the hospital bills, but this would not pay for the doctor bills, anesthesia, or medication. If I remember correctly, I was talking to my pastor's wife after my second surgery. I had expressed concern to her that I did not know where I was going to get money to pay for the medication I needed and pay for my medical bills. I guess that my needs were expressed to my church. I was still recovering from surgery and did not go to church for a couple of Sundays. It was at this time, without my knowledge, that my church took up two love offerings for me. Some members of my church came to visit me, and surprisingly blessed me with a check for over one thousand dollars. Tears just streamed down my face. I could not believe they would do this for me. God's love shined upon me through the loving financial gift from my church family. Receiving this financial gift was a humbling experience for me, because I wanted to be the giver, not the receiver. Throughout my life, I felt that a good bit of the time when some people would give me something or do something for me, they wanted something in return. But there were no strings attached to this freely given blessing. God was teaching me that it was okay to receive His blessings.

Continuing my Master's program, I did my internship for the counseling program at the Mental Health Department. It was at times extremely challenging. Working at Mental Health was a wonderful experience, and I learned so much. I had a great boss, and I worked with some highly skilled and wonderful people.

The fall semester began at Clemson, and I continued my assistantship. I began having some abnormal rectal bleeding. I called my gynecologist, and he referred me to my surgeon. I scheduled an appointment with her. I went for my appointment, and my surgeon did an examination. After the examination, she thought I had what she called a fistula. So, I was headed back to the hospital for exploratory surgery. After surgery, my surgeon said that I did not have a fistula, but something that was probably more like a cyst. I recovered.

The spring semester of 2000 was here. I would have a lot to do. I had to take a cumulative exit exam for my program and pass it to graduate. Also, I had to take the National

Certification Test for Counselors and pass it in order to get my license for counseling. The tests were pretty lengthy. There was only a month between tests. Having test anxiety, both tests would be a challenge.

Physically, I was still having rectal bleeding. Again, I contacted my surgeon to schedule an appointment. At the appointment, my surgeon scheduled a colonoscopy. The results from the colonoscopy showed that I had diverticulitis. This meant that my eating habits had to change even more, because there were even more foods I had to give up. My surgeon told me that my primary doctor would be able to help me with any problems I had with my diverticulitis. That day after my colonoscopy, I could hardly walk and was in serious pain. I already had an appointment scheduled with my physician for an asthma check-up the following week. I went to my scheduled appointment and let my doctor know the pain I was in. My doctor prescribed an antibiotic for me and off I went. I made some changes in my eating habits and did as my doctor prescribed. I did great for about a month. The rectal bleeding continued and appeared to get worse. I was having a lot of sharp pains down my left leg, swelling, and difficulty doing regular walking. Once again, I was headed back to my surgeon's office. My surgeon discussed with me my options for the diverticulitis. I decided that it would be best to go ahead and have the surgery. I scheduled surgery during the break between the spring semester 2000 and the summer session. My surgeon removed about twelve inches of my colon, and I no longer had diverticulitis. The surgery went well, and my recovery was great.

By this time, my little Eagle Summit car was running on its last legs. Around April of 2000, my car finally died. It was not worth repairing. Financially, I did not have the means to get a new car. I needed a car to get to and from work and school. At first, my pastor's family let me use their van for a month. Then, a lady from my church named Lynn told me she felt God told her to provide a car for me. Lynn told me that she would provide me with use of one of her cars for as long as I needed it. I was so amazed that people would freely offer me their cars with no strings attached. In August of 2000, I asked Lynn if I could purchase her Jeep that I was using. At first she said no, but later she called me to let me know she was interested in selling me the Jeep. Lynn and her husband called to let me know the price they were asking for the Jeep. I called my bank about getting a loan, but I would need a co-signer, because I did not have collateral. I let Lynn know that I needed a co-signer. Without hesitation she offered to co-sign for me, and I purchased her Jeep.

My days at Clemson were quickly coming to a close. I would take my last class in the first summer session of 2000. It was a psychopathology class. The professor was exceptionally hard. Also, being a summer school class it was very compact. But this would be the best class and hardest "A" that I had ever earned. Our professor gave a quiz almost every day. If you made an "A" in the class, then you would not have to take the final. And you know that I was praying every day for God to help me get that "A." Just before finals, our teacher gave us our grades to let us know who would be exempt from the final. According to him, I would have to take the final, but according to me I was exempt. So, after class I went up to him to let him know that I had made an "A." My teacher added up all my grades again, and I was right. My teacher had miscalculated my grade. I did get an "A," and I was exempt from the final. Our teacher told us that we were the best class that he had ever had. After class, my friend Cleat was waiting to see if I had to take the final. I went outside, and told him I did not have to take the final. Then, I got down on my knees right on the sidewalk and gave a big shout of thanks and praise to God. Cleat said someone was going to think I was bowing down to him, but I didn't care. What a great day it was, and a super ending to my final days at Clemson.

On August 12, 2000, I received my Master's degree from Clemson University. I graduated with a cumulative GPA of 3.81. Imagine that! Upon graduation, I was now a National Certified Counselor.

Throughout the many challenging physical and academic trials in my Master's program, God was faithful in each and every one. Academically, how amazing it was to make a 3.81 GPA. I strived for the 4.0 GPA. I think God had a purpose in my getting close to, but not attaining a 4.0 GPA. I believe that God's purpose was for me not to place my worth in a GPA.

After graduating from Clemson, I applied for a job with the Mental Health Department to be a Child and Adolescent Counselor. It would be a few weeks before I would know that I got the job. On July 15, 2000, I received word that I got the job. I was excited. My job at Clemson had already ended, and it would be a month before I would receive my first paycheck. Financially, things were still tight. I had all kinds of medical bills to start paying. Also, I was going to have to start making payments on my school loans, but I would be able to defer the payments for a while. Again, the Lord provided me with a financial blessing from some friends.

Physically, I was having a problem. Again, I was having abnormal vaginal bleeding and pain. So, once again I was off to see my gynecologist. I told my doctor about the problems I was having. He decided to try medication to see if it would correct the problem. However, this did not work, and in time the problem got worse. In December of 2000, I went back for my appointment with Dr. R.; I let him know that something was really wrong with me. Dr. R. agreed to do exploratory surgery to see if he could find out what the problem was. At the time, Dr. R. felt that I might have endometriosis, but I told him that I didn't have endometriosis, because it just wasn't me. Dr. R. scheduled my surgery.

On January 16, 2001, I was scheduled to have exploratory laser surgery. I had surgery. That evening, Dr. R. came to check on me in the hospital. He said I told him something was wrong, and it was really wrong. Dr. R. said that he went in with a laser, but he could not find my left ovary, so he had to cut my stomach open. Dr. R. said that the scar tissue from my colon surgery covered and attached my left ovary underneath my colon. Dr. R. said that he had to remove my left ovary and tube. Dr. R. said that it was a long and hard surgery for him. Dr. R. said that I did not meet the criteria to be officially diagnosed with endometriosis, which was great. The good news was that I had medical insurance this time. My hospital stay would be longer than I had expected, but I would fully recover.

My job working at the Mental Health Department was definitely an adjustment, but I loved my children. However, I did not care for the company I worked for. I felt that the company did not care for the clients or the employees, and I did not agree with some of the things the company did. The majority of the children I had seen for counseling services were from the lower socioeconomic class and some did not have money or insurance for services. This was very hard for me, because I wanted to help them. Although I loved the experience I was getting working at Mental Health, I was not happy. I started pursuing other avenues for job opportunities.

My asthma problem was not doing well. For the second time in the past six months, I had an upper respiratory infection. My asthma was very severe. I was now taking the highest dosage of medication that my doctor could prescribe for me, and I was taking breathing treatments. At one point, my doctor even considered hospitalizing me, because my asthma was so severe. As time went on, my asthma symptoms subsided. I did pray that God would heal me from this asthma. In January of 2001, I noticed that I was forgetting to take my asthma medication. Then, I noticed that I was able to breathe just fine without the medication. So, I took myself off the asthma medication completely. I believed God totally healed me of asthma. I have not taken any medication since then, and I have not had any more asthma symptoms at all.

Physically, I began to notice I was extremely tired. I was having much difficulty staying awake, especially while driving, and maybe was a little emotionally sensitive. My body was in pain from head to toe, and it was difficult for me to get out of bed in the morning. I did not know what was wrong with me. I didn't feel that I was depressed, because there was nothing that I had to be depressed about. That summer of 2001, I went to see my gynecologist for my annual routine check-up. I told Dr. R. that I had been very tired and had much physical pain. Dr. R. recommended medication for depression, much to my surprise. I had no idea that once again I would be suffering with depression. Anyway, I agreed to take the medication, but I did not like some of the side effects of the medication. Eventually, I took myself off the medication, and I am trusting God to completely heal me soon and free me from the bondage of depression.

I was still pursuing other job opportunities, in particular in the school system. I have wanted to work in the school setting, because I felt that I could help the children for free. A job position came open for a guidance counselor in the high school setting, in the summer of 2001. I applied for the job, but I was required to take a Praxis II test. The Praxis II was a required test for guidance counseling. I did not feel I could pass this test, so I withdrew my name. Also, I knew that I would have to go back to school and take several more classes for guidance counseling, because this was not my specific field of study. At this time, I was not sure that I wanted to go back to school.

That fall of 2001, I was denied a raise from the company, because they said that I had not met their requirements for a raise. I was so angry, because I felt that I had worked very hard at my job. Also, I felt that I had contributed to helping improve the company and its relations with other community resources. I felt I deserved the raise. Now, I really wanted another job, and I was looking.

In January of 2002, there was an immediate opening for a guidance counselor at the high school level again. My application was still on file in the school system, so I just called and said that I was interested in the job. I still had to take the required Praxis II test. On Monday evening, January 7, 2002, I found out that the Praxis II was going to be given at the local college in town. The test date was Saturday, January 12. I registered to take the Praxis II test. I did not have time to go out and find material to study for the test or to study. I was just trusting God for this one. Saturday came and with a lot of prayer I went and took the test. Some weeks later, I got the results from the Praxis II. I had passed the test. Some time later I saw a friend of mine and was telling her about my taking the Praxis II test and passing it. In amazement, she told me that she had a friend who took a year's sabbatical, just to prepare for that test. And I just went and took it. Well, I didn't have anytime to even think about it, let alone prepare for it.

I called the Human Resource person, Ms. B. in the school system to notify her that I had passed the Praxis II test. Ms. B informed me that the counseling position had already been filled. I was so upset. Ms. B. told me to keep checking, because usually when they hire in a situation such as this was, the job position would reopen at the end of the semester. So, I kept checking, and sure enough the school system was taking applications for the high school counselor position. My application was still valid, and I made sure I did all the necessary things I needed to in applying for the position. I got a call to interview for the counseling position. I went to the interview and I thought it went very well, but someone else got the position. I was very disappointed. Again, I talked with Ms. B., and she said that there was possibly another position that would be open that she thought that I would like better. I was adamant and persistent in pursuing this job. I kept calling to check on the status of the job opening. A counseling position was now open for the Alternative School. Since I was not certified for guidance counseling, I called the State Education Department to find out if there was anything else I needed to do to be qualified for the guidance position. The lady I spoke to at the time said the state would be requiring guidance counselors to not only take the Praxis II, but also the Praxis I. Plus, I already knew that I would have to take some classes for guidance counseling to get certified. As for the Praxis I, I would cross that bridge when I came to it.

In May of 2002, I called Ms. B. in the school system to inquire about the counseling job again. I let her know about the information I got from the lady at the State Department regarding the requirements for certification for guidance counseling. I believe when I talked to Ms. B. that day, she told me that she had received a letter from the state department. Ms. B. said that the letter said something to the effect that the state was now recognizing National Certified Counselors to be qualified for the guidance counseling certification. I was not exactly sure what this news meant, but I was going to have to be hired first before I could apply for certification. At this time, I was in the process of getting my license for professional counseling. I persisted in getting an interview for the job at the Alternative School. Finally, in the beginning of July of 2002, I got my long-awaited interview. When I left the interview, I really did not feel I would get this job. I knew that there were many people that applied for the job that were already certified, experienced, and trained in guidance counseling. A few weeks had passed, and I had not heard any word from Ms. B. regarding my status for getting the job. I did not call her either. I felt that if God wanted me to have the job, He would give it to me. I remember every time I passed by the school where the job opening was, or even the street it was on I claimed that job. I said something like "Thank you, God, for my job." The new school year was getting ready to begin. Exactly two weeks and one day before the day school opened, I got a call on a Tuesday night from Ms. B., but I was not home. Ms. B. left a message on my answering machine saying that I got the job at the Alternative School, and she wanted to know if I was still interested. Was I ever interested! I was so excited. I could not believe that I was selected for the job. I did not know that I was even being considered for the position. I finished listening to the message, but Ms. B. did not leave a number where I could contact her that night. A short time later the phone rang, and it was Ms. B. Again, Ms. B. let me know that I got the job, and did I still want it. Elated, I told her that I was still interested in the job, and I gratefully accepted. Ms. B. told me that I had to come to the office as soon as possible to complete some paper work. I was there the next morning, before I had to be at work. Ms. B. gave me further direction as to what I needed to do. That day, I would resign my position as Child and Adolescent Counselor at Mental Health to take the guidance counselor position at the school. I was able to give my boss exactly a two-week notice, just in time to be able to start the new school year. What an answer to prayer, and such a blessing this job opportunity would be. Now, I would be able to counsel and help the children free of charge to them.

Now that I was hired, I was able to apply for certification for guidance counselor. I sent all my information to the State Education Department to be approved for certification. The State gave me a conditional certification. The condition was that I had to take a class and pass it. The class was one that was required of all new employees in the district.

Upon completing the class, the State gave me a clear, renewable certification for guidance counseling. This meant that there were no other requirements that I had to meet. I was certified.

This job would bring about many new changes and challenges for me, especially in the area of speaking and writing proper English and grammar. For example, I had to write teacher memos and letters to parents. This was my biggest adjustment and challenge. I was absolutely not a letter writer. There were not enough words in my vocabulary to write a letter. However, I bought some resource books to help me write letters properly. And my boss was great in helping me adjust to my new challenges. As time passes, I am getting better at letter writing, and all the other things I have had to learn. I am feeling more comfortable with my job, but every day I am learning new things. I still love the children and I pray that God will continue to help me improve myself to be better able to help and serve the children. During this time, I was able to complete all requirements for my license in counseling. On November 18, 2003, I received a letter of notification that I was granted a license for professional counseling. Just recently, I have I received notification that I am certified in anger management (Certified Anger Management Specialist). God was surely working all things together for good!

Chapter 7

The Promised Land

"Consider it all joy, my brethren, when you encounter
various trials, knowing that the testing of your faith
produces endurance. And let endurance have its perfect
result that you may be perfect, and complete, lacking
nothing." James 1:2-4

As a young child the story of Moses fascinated me. God
chose Moses to serve Him, and lead the children of
Israel out of Egypt to the Promised Land. Now, Moses was a
simple man who had a speech problem. The Bible says that
Moses had a stuttering problem. He was far from perfect and
even a murderer. Moses was an unlikely candidate chosen
by God to speak to Pharaoh to let His people go. And yet,
God sent Him, and He fully equipped Moses to get the job
done. Throughout the Bible, God chose some of the most
unlikely people to do great things for Him. And I am just
an ordinary, yet simple woman carrying a suitcase full of
emotional baggage from my past. But, I believe that I am
one of God's chosen people chosen by God to be "A Most
Unlikely Servant."

I remember when I was a young child; my sister Jean took me and a few other brothers and sisters to see the movie *The Ten Commandments*. The movie captured my heart. My favorite part of the movie was when Moses came down off the mountain after being with God. I was so intrigued, and captivated by Moses' transformation. He was a changed man, and he looked so distinguished. Moses' face was luminous and glimmering with sheer radiance. My eyes photographed that picture of transformation and etched it in my mind and heart forever. Remembering that day in the movie theater, I so wanted to feel like Moses looked. I desired that mountaintop experience. The scene where Moses came down from the mountain made me want to climb right up that mountain, and come down a changed person, just like Moses.

The story goes on to tell how the children of Israel spent forty years wandering in the desert. Even with Israel's newfound freedom, they complained, grumbled, and were ungrateful, because they felt God was not supplying their needs. As I am now in my early forties, I can relate to the children of Israel. Sometimes, I feel like I have spent forty years wandering in the desert trying to get to my promised land, many times complaining and grumbling, thinking that God has forgotten about me. At times, I would just look up toward the heavens and give a big shout to God saying; "Hey, did you forget about me?" By the way, waiting on God or being patient is not one of my strong points, but I am learning. Sometimes, just my own disobedience to God has held me back. And my disobedience to God only proved to make me have some huge setbacks and caused me even more pain. You think that I would get this right after a while, but sometimes I still struggle. Then, God gives me the strength to pick myself up and keep pressing on.

You see, I have been on both sides of the world, being born and raised Catholic and now being a Christian. As I believe I said earlier, I do not feel that my religious upbringing was detrimental to my spiritual growth, because I believe that God's hand was on me. For example, one time while I was doing my undergraduate studies, I was talking to one of my professors. I am sure I was seeking some type of guidance from him. I remember telling him about my Catholic upbringing. Our conversation then went something like this; my professor asked me if I believed that Mary, the mother of Jesus, was a virgin all her life. I told him no. My professor said that he has never talked to a person who was Catholic that did not believe the Mary, Jesus' mother, was a virgin all her life. I guess I missed that part of the Catholic teaching. Anyway, I remember telling my professor that I honored Mary, because she was Jesus' mother. The Bible clearly states that Jesus had brothers and sisters.

If someone were to ask me if I would change anything about my life, without hesitation, I would say no. I would not change anything, because all the things I went through have made me and are helping me to become the person I am today. Some of the choices I made that proved to be good choices would have not been good had my circumstances been different. For instance, if I had a slender, skinny body or good self-image of myself when I was younger, I probably would have led a sexually promiscuous life style. Then, I may have not known the truth about being raped. If I had multiple sex partners, then I might have not known that I actually got an STD from being raped. If I would have married when I was younger, I do not deem I would have made a good wife or mother. I believe that not having dealt with all my abuse and emotional problems would have interfered with my being able to be a good wife and mother. I feel that my anger, even though I turned it inward, would have interfered with my everyday living, and my functioning role as a wife and mother. The fact of the matter is that my denial of my abuse issues affected my awareness that I even had a problem.

Along time ago, in an article from *Our Daily Bread*, a Christian devotional booklet. I found a story about wounded oysters that touched my heart. The article says that:

> "Each pearl is formed by an oyster's internal response to a wound cause by an irritant, such as a grain of sand. Resources of repair rush to the injured area. The final result is a lustrous pearl. Something beautiful is created that would have been impossible without the wound."

I feel like that wounded oyster, but God has taken my wounded and injured soul, and is turning me into something beautiful. I want to be God's pearl. In Psalm 119:71a it says; "It is good for me that I was afflicted...." My affliction was good, because it gave me the strength and courage to leave behind a life that was going nowhere, a life that was being wasted and slowly withering away.

Throughout my life, God has placed many wonderful people in my path to help me along the way to get me one step closer to Him. Even in sickness, God gave me the most wonderfully caring and attentive doctors. There were many twists, turns, detours, and dead ends along the road I have traveled, but the Lord has been teaching me many things during my journey. The Lord is teaching me that the moments or things that used to define my self-worth were just that. In Romans 8:31 it says; "If God is for us, who can be against us?" The Lord loves me just as I am, and I am His child. The Lord is teaching me to trust and depend on Him to provide and meet all my needs. A long time ago, way before I left Pittsburgh, I used to play the lottery. I did not play the lottery every day, and I think that I probably won more than I paid into it, or was about even. One day I got to thinking that all the money I had was God's money, and I felt that playing the lottery was not what I needed to do, so

I quit. Even when I won the lottery, I didn't have any more money than I had before. It quickly disappeared. It just gave a false sense of security.

God has pretty much emptied my suitcase of emotional baggage. He has done some miraculous healing in me. He is mending my heart and soul more and more every day. The memories of my abuse do not consume my every thought anymore; as a matter of fact some things I just do not even give thought to. God has provided for me in my times of need. Just recently, I have finished paying off all the medical bills I had from all the surgeries without medical insurance. What praise to God! And I am learning to become more dependent on Him.

Something I like to do is thank God for His favor. Every day I say, "Thank you God that I will find favor everywhere I go." This is so much fun. For example, when I go to the grocery store, I find a lot of food items that I buy marked down to a very low sale price. I am a bargain shopper, and I get so excited when I get a bargain. I could pretty much say that the majority of the time, I do find favor everywhere I go. I love finding favor with God and getting so many blessings. Even more fun is the perfect peace I have when I am following God's will and allowing Him to direct my paths.

A lot of times, people go searching for something or someone tangible or something to give them hope, such as good luck charms or psychics. I did. I said earlier that I got into psychics and astrology, because it gave me hope, and something to believe in. But now my hope is in Jesus Christ, because He lives within my heart. In I Peter 3:15 it says: "Always be prepared to give an answer to everyone who asks you to give the reason for the hope that you have...." And I can give an answer. I can say without a doubt that there is no better way to live in this world, than to have Jesus in your heart. Let me say here that living a life in Jesus does not promise that you will never experience any suffering or pain. As a matter of fact, you may face more adversity and trials than you ever had before. I have weathered many storms in my life, but God has made the Son to shine upon me. The happiness that I went searching for a long time ago could not be found in money, people, or materialistic things. I learned that true happiness is found within my heart in the love of the Lord. And happiness can only be felt when you have that perfect peace that only the Lord Jesus Christ can give. The joy of the Lord that decorates my heart now does not compare with anything the world has to offer.

As I strive to become more like Christ, He is turning my thoughts and desires toward Him. My desires for the things of the world are quickly fading and more distant with each passing day. God has given me an awesome vision for my life. I know that I am camping right outside the gate of my promised land. I am just waiting for God to swing open the gates, and let me through. That awesome vision God gave me for my life, I believe that He will soon bring to pass.

My prayer is to showcase the beautiful gifts and talents that the Lord has blessed me with, to be a light so that when people meet me and look into my eyes they would see the love of the Lord within my heart and the desire for the better life in Jesus. A life in Jesus comes with an eternal warranty for life with satisfaction guaranteed. Let the Lord be your soul's provider and reap the great benefits with a heavenly reward. Jesus is the only way to heaven. God tells us in John 3:16 that; "For God so loved the world, that He gave His only begotten Son, that whoever believes in Him should not perish, but have eternal life."

If you have never received Jesus in your heart, I would like to invite you to do so by praying this prayer; "Dear Lord, please forgive me for my sins, for I am a sinner. I believe Jesus died on the cross for my sins. I ask you to come into my heart, and be the Lord and Savior of my life. In Jesus' name I pray, Amen." Is Jesus knocking on the door of your heart? Will you let Him in or turn Him away? I pray that your decision will be to let Him in.

"Truly, Truly, I say to you, he who hears My word, and believes Him who sent Me, has eternal life, and does not come into judgment, but has passed out of death into life." John 5:24

Printed in the United States
62702LVS00001B/271-417

9 781600 345210